Series / Number 07-063

SURVEY QUESTIONS

Handcrafting the
Standardized Questionnaire

JEAN M. CONVERSE
University of Michigan

STANLEY PRESSER
National Science Foundation

SAGE PUBLICATIONS
The International Professional Publishers
Newbury Park   London   New Delhi

For information address:

SAGE Publications, Inc.
2455 Teller Road
Thousand Oaks, California 91320
E-mail: order@sagepub.com

SAGE Publications Ltd.
6 Bonhill Street
London EC2A 4PU
United Kingdom

SAGE Publications India Pvt. Ltd.
M-32 Market
Greater Kailash I
New Delhi 110 048 India

International Standard Book Number 978-0-8039-2743-8

Library of Congress Catalog Card No. 85-061665

14 13 12 11   28 27 26 25

When citing a university paper, please use the proper form. Remember to cite the correct
Sage University Paper series title and include the paper number. One of the following
formats can be adapted (depending on the style manual used):

(1) IVERSEN, GUDMUND R. and NORPOTH, HELMUT (1976) "Analysis of
Variance." Sage University Paper series on Quantitative Applications in the Social Sciences,
07-001. Beverly Hills, CA: Sage Publications.

OR

(2) Iversen, Gudmund R., and Norpoth, Helmut. 1996. *Analysis of Variance*. Sage
University Paper series on Quantitative Applications in the Social Sciences, series no.
07-001). Beverly Hills, CA: Sage Publications.

CONTENTS

SERIES EDITOR'S INTRODUCTION

It has been 35 years since the first publication of Stanley Payne's classic work in survey question design, *The Art of Asking Questions* (Princeton: Princeton University Press, 1951). The present volume, *Survey Questions: Handcrafting the Standardized Questionnaire*, is a worthy heir to the Payne tradition. It shares his view that question writing must be guided not only by intuition and experience but also by the evidence of rigorous experiment. Payne pointed repeatedly to the need for quantitative evidence upon which to base this art, but experimental work into questions nevertheless languished until the 1970s.

Recent research has yielded many new clues about how survey questions "behave," and some of these findings have offered practical guidance on question writing. In the present book, Converse and Presser have reviewed this experimental literature, as well as the lore of professional experience, and culled from them those guiding principles and specific findings that have some strong implications for how to write survey questions. Mindful that the findings of experiments cannot be applied mechanically and that survey questions cannot be mass-produced, they have suggested a number of ways in which to make pilot and pretest work more fruitful. This is all the more impressive because they have done so with wit and with grace. The material they have presented is easily accessible and yet professionally sophisticated— precisely the balance we hope to achieve with the monographs in this series.

We are therefore especially pleased to add this volume to our burgeoning list of monographs. It is a particularly nice complement to Kalton's volume (number 35 in this series) on survey sampling, to the volume by Kiecolt and Nathan (number 53 in the series) on the secondary analysis of survey data, and to the Fox and Tracy volume on randomized response (number 58 in the series). We hope to add additional volumes on survey research, including an introduction to CATI (Computer Assisted Telephone Interviewing) and other relevant topics. Ultimately, the series should provide sufficient materials upon which to build a complete introduction to survey research, for both the beginning practitioner and the classroom instructor.

—John L. Sullivan
Series Co-Editor

PREFACE

This book is based on the premise that surveys must be custom-built to the specification of given research purposes. Yet it is unrewarding to be told, always, that writing questions is simply an art. It is surely that, but there are also some guidelines that have emerged from the collective artistic experience and the collective research tradition. We have arranged these ideas in three classes, or concentric circles, which progressively narrow to the specific design task, and we have written this book in three chapters to match.

Chapter 1 bears on general strategies culled from examples or experience of question-crafters and the findings of empirical researchers. In one sense, this material is a litany of cautions, offering more general perspectives than specific procedures. We hope that Chapter 1 presents something of the judicial or "research temper" as applied to survey questions.

Chapter 2 focuses on specific empirical findings. In recent years, there has been renewed research into question design and question effects, and much has been learned about how some questions tend to "behave." But the implications of this research for actual practice are not always clear. In this chapter we have selected those research findings that seem to us to have fairly direct applicability.

Chapter 3 tries to zero in on the actual task at hand. It is about pilot work and pretesting and making use of the advice of experts—critics, colleagues, and especially interviewers. It is commonplace that all survey questions must be pretested, but there is no commonly shared "tradition" about how to go about it. We have found only a very few references bearing on the subject. In this chapter we hope to contribute to the building of such a tradition.

Throughout this book we draw upon our own research experience as well as upon the published literature and the experience relayed by colleagues. Because we have had more personal experience with face-to-face and telephone interviewing than with written questionnaires, we make few extensions to that third mode of administration. Our

8

experience is focused in still another way. We are most familiar with questionnaires designed for use with the broad American public— national cross-section samples drawn by the Institute for Social Research, or samples of the greater Detroit metropolitan area by the Detroit Area Study (both of the University of Michigan). We have had only a very little experience with surveying the well educated or intensely motivated such as college students, legislators, social scientists, political activists, and medical patients; some of the cautions that we urge in Chapter 1, especially, may well not apply to questionnaire design for these special groups.

Who will find this book of value? We hope that it will be useful to practitioners trying to handcraft their own questionnaires, and to students, and instructors in graduate and undergraduate teaching of survey research and social science methods. For professional survey researchers with years of practical experience and a rich knowledge of the research literature, this book can only remind rather than instruct.

We are grateful for the interest and editorial criticism of Howard Schuman, the original prime mover of this project. We also thank Tracy R. Berckmans, Robert M. Groves, Lee Sigelman, Charles F. Turner, Sage Publications editors John L. Sullivan and Richard G. Niemi, and two anonymous reviewers for their many good suggestions. These counselors are of course innocent of all failings that remain in the book.

SURVEY QUESTIONS: HANDCRAFTING THE STANDARDIZED QUESTIONNAIRE

JEAN M. CONVERSE
University of Michigan

STANLEY PRESSER
National Science Foundation

1. STRATEGIES OF EXPERIENCE AND RESEARCH

The Enduring Counsel for Simplicity

Surveys and polls have become a staple of American cultural life in the course of the past 40-50 years. There are now burgeoning archives of survey data—banks of questions, whole studies to be replicated, imitated, or adapted to new purposes—but models of ideal question practice are nevertheless still hard to come by. Replication itself may be a weak reed. Even if we carefully select questions that have been used before, we cannot be sure that the original questions were good ones in the first place; and even if they were, new bugs may have gotten into old questions, as language and the world moved on.

We are better advised to start with two more general perspectives: the experience of master question-writers and the general strategies distilled by empirical researchers (these people are sometimes one and the same). Just as these social scientists cannot anticipate all the varied *functions* of the research that we plan, so they cannot instruct us unerringly in our question *forms*. Their insights will often be rather general and we will have to make such applications as we can to the research at hand.

We find convergence in their counsel, nonetheless. Question-crafters tend to speak of the need for simplicity, intelligibility, clarity. The experimental researchers, striving for more abstraction, tend to refer to "task difficulty" and the properties of questions that are likely to add to "respondent burden" (Babbie, 1973; Bradburn, 1983; Bradburn and Sudman, 1979; Hoinville and Jowell, 1978; Kahn and Cannell, 1957; Kornhauser and Sheatsley, 1976; Maccoby and Maccoby, 1954; Payne, 1951; Sheatsley, 1983; Sudman and Bradburn, 1982). But these two sets of preoccupations are highly overlapping with similar implications for the handcrafting of survey questions. They both point to the fact that questionnaires are often difficult to understand and to answer. As Sheatsley (1983: 200) observes,

> Because questionnaires are usually written by educated persons who have a special interest in and understanding of the topic of their inquiry, and because these people usually consult with other educated and concerned persons, it is much more common for questionnaires to be overwritten, overcomplicated, and too demanding of the respondent than they are to be simpleminded, superficial, and not demanding enough.

This means, in turn, that writing sufficiently clear and "simple" questions is hard-won, heavy-duty work for survey researchers. It requires special measures to cast questions that are clear and straightforward in four important respects: simple language, common concepts, manageable tasks, and widespread information.

SIMPLE LANGUAGE

Speaking in common tongues

Speaking the common language means finding synonyms for the polysyllabic and Latinate constructions that come easily to the tongue of the college educated. One need not, usually, say "principal" because "main" will do as well. "Intelligible" is rarely as good as "clear" or "understandable." "Intuitive" (or "counterintuitive") has taken a leading place in the special vocabulary of social scientists, but it is a pretentious choice if "feeling" carries essentially the same meaning.

Although the number of syllables in a question is not a perfect indicator of the complexity or the difficulty of words, it is a good place to start being wary. One may want to check suspicious words against published frequency counts of American vocabulary, to try to cut "elevated" language down to the size of the plainer-spoken alternative (Carroll et al., 1973; Dahl, 1979; Kučera and Francis, 1967). These volumes have stringent limitations, however, for they tally the literal appearance of a word, not the frequency of its use in all its special meanings. We have learned more from talking, listening, and pretesting than from reference books of this kind.

Must questions be written in standard English? Yes, almost always, but not necessarily standard *written* English or a grammar teacher's special tongue. The standard may be *spoken* English, for indeed in the face-to-face and telephone interview, these questions will be spoken by an interviewer. We feel that it is legitimate to violate certain conventions of written English if the pure construction sounds stilted or pretentious. For example, other writers on question design have recently made use of this item: "Physical fitness is an idea the time of which has come" (Fink and Kosecoff, 1985: 38). For our part, we would either use the unadulterated cliché, "an idea whose time has come," or abandon the item. But these details are finally matters of taste. There is consensus on the broader view that questions should be in straightforward language— not chatty, overfamiliar, or cast in some subculture's slang.

Must questions be short?

The counsel to keep questions short has been qualified by research and experience of recent years. In 1951, Payne was convinced that one should aspire to asking questions that numbered no more than around twenty words (Payne, 1951: 136). Under some conditions, however, length appears to be a virtue. In an experimental study of health measures, for example, more symptoms were reported by respondents when longer questions were asked. In the standard version, respondents were asked such questions as, "What medicines, if any, did you take or use during the past 4 weeks?" In a redundant version, questions were lengthened with "filler" words designed to add no new information as in this example: "The next question is about medicines during the past 4 weeks. We want to ask you about this. What medicines, if any, did you take or use during the past 4 weeks?" (Henson et al., 1979; Laurent, 1972).

It is not yet entirely clear what is going on in these experiments. The additional material spoken by the interviewer may stimulate the respondent to talk more, and this additional talk may aid the respondent's recall too (Sudman and Bradburn, 1982: 50-51). On the other hand, the extra material may simply give the respondent more time to think; and there is indeed ample evidence that interviewers tend to go too fast (Cannell et al., 1979).

These results about longer questions are evocative but still somewhat ambiguous. One should consider the use of redundancy now and then to introduce new topics and also to flesh out single questions, but if one larded all questions with "filler" phrases, a questionnaire would soon be bloated with too few, too fat questions. In any case, the more important strategy may be attacking the issue of interviewer pace directly and instituting special training to slow interviewers down.

In other cases, long questions or introductions may be necessary to communicate the nature of the task. In the so-called feeling thermometer used by the National Election Study (NES), each specific question is brief:

> Our first person is Jimmy Carter.
> How would you rate him using the thermometer?

But the introduction is a massive 140 words:

> I'd like to get your feelings toward some of our political leaders and other people who are in the news these days. I'll read the name of a person and I'd like you to rate that person using this feeling thermometer. You may use any number from 0 to 100 for a rating. Ratings between 50 and 100 degrees mean that you feel favorable and warm toward the person. Ratings between 0 and 50 degrees mean that you don't feel too favorable toward the person. If we come to a person whose name you don't recognize, you don't need to rate that person. Just tell me and we'll move on to the next one. If you do recognize the name, but don't feel particularly warm or cold toward the person, you would rate that person at the 50 degree mark [Miller et al., 1982: 86].

Despite its length, the thermometer question seems to be clear to respondents because of the familiar image of this measuring device.

These long questions cannot be faulted as generically "bad examples," for they have been put into useful service. Beginners writing their own, original questions are probably well-advised nonetheless to heed Payne's counsel for brevity. The best strategy is doubtless to use short questions when possible and slow interviewer delivery—always—so that respondents have time to think.

Some avoidable confusions

Double vision. Counsel against using the "double-barreled" question is ubiquitous. One form of the offender is usually pretty easy to spot ("Do you think women and children should be given the first available flu shots?"), and we need not discuss it further. Another form has often been identified with the problem of "prestige," when a policy issue is identified with a public figure, for example, President Reagan's policy on Nicaragua. Such a question has two attitudinal objects—the president and the policy—so it too can be considered a less obvious form of the double-barreled question. It may be treated as two separate questions, in a split sample comparison, or it may be considered an indissoluble double stimulus, in which the policy is not fully identifiable without the association of the president.

Double *negatives,* however, are much to be avoided; they can introduce a needless confusion and they can creep in unobserved. Consider this Agree/Disagree item:

Please tell me whether you agree or disagree with the following statement about teachers in the public schools:

Teachers should not be required to supervise students in the halls, the lunchroom, and school parking lots.

Agree   Disagree

One may Agree that teachers should not be required to do this kind of duty outside of the classroom. But the Disagree side gets tangled, for it means "I do not think that teachers should not be required to supervise students outside of their classrooms"—that is, teachers should be required. Such a question can slip into a list when investigators have not read aloud and *listened* carefully to all the questions in the series. Such difficulties raise the issue, which we discuss in Chapter 2, of whether or not Agree/Disagree items should be used at all. But if they are considered essential, one should try to cast them as positive statements.

Implicit negatives—mispronounced. It is also possible that the negative meaning conveyed by words such as *control, restrict, forbid, ban, outlaw, restrain, oppose,* lends itself to confusion. If these "restrictive" words get attached to questions involving positive notions about freedom and liberty, it may not be clear whether respondents are for restricting *free* trade or restricting *trade.* One should be on the lookout for this kind of problem, even though little research bears directly on the point and written illustrations of it may not be compelling. It may seem far-fetched, for example, that words so opposite in meaning as these two might be confused:

- Do you favor or oppose a law *outlawing* guns in the state of Maryland?
- Do you favor or oppose a law *allowing* guns in the state of Maryland?

Still, it is important to remember that when respondents are listening to questions, not reading them, they are entirely reliant on what interviewers say, and if a key word *is* mispronounced or mumbled by an interviewer, it will probably be misheard or misinterpreted by the respondent. The experience of monitoring telephone interviews can—and should—make investigators vigilant to anticipate the likelier distortions and avoid them, if possible, by choosing words that are more difficult to confuse.

Overlong lists. The use of printed aids in the personal interview is probably a good deal more common than it was in early days of survey research. Respondents now are often given a "show card" to read that spells out the alternatives to a question. Certainly anything as complex as Kohn's (1969) list of thirteen qualities that might be considered desirable in a child—such as:

- that a child has good manners
- that a child has good sense and sound judgment
- that a child is responsible

—would typically be designed for simultaneous presentation in two forms: oral presentation by the interviewer and silent reading by the respondent. It is often the case that even simpler sets of four or five alternatives such as Very Often, Frequently, Seldom, and Hardly Ever will be read aloud by the interviewer and also made available in written form on a card or a small booklet for the respondent's reference. This is highly desirable practice. It is not helpful for illiterates, to be sure—and interviewers should be trained to be sensitive to that situation—but it seems to represent a convenient review for everyone else. We know of no research on the point but common sense appears to have made "show cards" a common technique.

Dangling alternatives. Asking response alternatives before introducing the topic itself, such as "Would you say that it is very often, frequently, seldom, or hardly ever that...." is a difficult construction; it demands that the respondent keep these unattached alternatives in mind before knowing what topic to fix them to. The subject matter must come first; then the respondent can consider matters of degree or frequency: "How often do you and your husband disagree about spending money: very often, frequently, seldom, or hardly ever?" is the preferred order.

COMMON CONCEPTS

Making questions conceptually clear may be the most difficult assignment for social scientists, for they are usually rather charmed by abstract thinking in the first place, and then are trained in its pleasures. They lose touch with how difficult abstractions can be if one is not accustomed to moving them around in the mind. Mathematical abstractions tend to be difficult for the general public—and even for some people who are highly educated by not in mathematics or statistics.

"Variance" for instance—survey researchers would not think of asking the general public questions about variances or standard deviations. They know perfectly well that the concept of an average, or a mean, is much more widely understood than the concept of variability about that mean, or measures of dispersion. (Even statistically inclined baseball fans, avid about batting averages, are less likely to understand short-term variability in batting performances, and will cheer the streaks and boo the slumps.) Although survey researchers wisely avoid variance, they occasionally use concepts that are no less difficult.

Rates of change, for instance, bear on concepts that are formalized in calculus—not the stuff of everyday culture. This question was asked of a national sample in recent years:

Compared to a year ago, do you feel the prices of most things you buy are going up faster than they did then, going up as fast, going up slower, or not going up at all [Harris and Associates, 1970: 157]?

Mark that this is not simply asking whether or not prices are going up. It asks the respondent to compare the rate at which prices are going up this year with the rate they went up last year. Note too that although the question is full of short words—there is not a real polysyllable in it—it is still a very difficult question. It was duly answered by almost everyone in the national sample—only 2% said that they were Not Sure; 72% said that prices this year were going up faster than last year—and probably because respondents simplified it to comment not on comparative rates but simply current rise of prices.

There is a little evidence that even concepts that seem a good deal easier, such as percentages and proportions, are not handled well by much of the general public. In a study by Belson (1981: 244-245), respondents were asked what meaning they had given to various questions, such as "What proportion of your evening viewing time do you spend watching news programmes?" Only 14 of 53 respondents understood proportion as "part," "fraction," or "percentage." About one third of the others interpreted the term in a broadly quantitative sense (such as how long, how many hours, how often). A larger group interpreted the question to tap other dimensions entirely—*when* they watched, *which* programs, even which channel. Belson suspects that a substantial proportion of people do not understand the meaning of the word itself, and that another set, who probably do understand it, tend to avoid the difficulty of working it out.

That sounds like a splendid reason for not asking such a question. There is enough work for respondents to do in totting up their own total listening behavior (assuming that it is quite regular) and then adding up the news programs—without asking for a proportion, too. Far better to ask the respondent two or three simpler questions, on total listening time and on news-listening, on this order:

- In the past week, (SINCE DATE OR DAY) how many hours did you watch television in the evening?
- Did you spend any of that time watching any news programs? (IF YES) How many hours did you watch news programs?

And let investigators calculate the proportion themselves!

MANAGEABLE TASKS

Meaning: the fact/attitude divide

Is it easier for respondents to answer questions of personal fact—questions bearing on their own experience and behavior—than to respond to questions about opinions and attitudes? From a common-sense standpoint, it might seem so. Questions of personal fact, after all, refer to a physical or social reality: whether one is married or not married; whether one went to work yesterday or stayed home in bed with the flu; what one's job is and what paycheck it yields; and so on.

In recent years, survey questions of "fact" have come under new scrutiny, as the boundary between facts and attitudes has been shown to be sometimes a vague and permeable one. For example, as Smith (1984b) has pointed out, ethnicity is often left to the respondent's own subjective definition ("What do you consider your main ethnic or nationality group?") because respondents may have a large collection of birthplaces in their genealogy or lack the relevant information. Being unemployed is another example of a subjectively defined fact, for it incorporates the notion of "looking for work," a phrase that might mean anything from pounding the pavement to looking out the window. The measure of unemployment used by the federal government's Current Population Survey includes any of these activities—anything, in fact, except "nothing"—so it is the respondent who defines what "looking for work" means.

"Facts" of this sort can hardly be distinguished from attitudes, and may be prey to the kinds of ambiguities of meaning and frame of reference that attitude questions are. Recent work for the National Crime Survey shows ambiguities in the definitions of crime, for example. In an experimental study designed to broaden respondents' frame of reference for criminal victimization, a debriefing was held with respondents. They were presented with six different vignettes and asked whether or not each one was "the type of crime we are interested in, in this survey." Results showed that the experimental questionnaire had been effective in certain respects but was not wholly successful in matching respondents' and investigators' definitions of reportable crime. For example, the theft of an office typewriter from "Mary's" desk at work was included by about 90% of respondents, although this was not considered in scope by the investigators because the survey was to cover only personal and household belongings. On the other hand, assault by

"Jean's" husband—he slapped her hard across the face and chipped her tooth—was not deemed a crime by about 25% of the respondents (Martin 1986: 32-33). The current attention to spouse and child abuse turns on the last point especially: The effort to give criminal status to behaviors that have been excluded from that definition when the victims were family members (Cowan et al., 1978; Skogan, 1981).

As Martin (1986: 4) points out, however, ambiguity and subjectivity cannot be eliminated entirely from crime reporting:

> For all classes of [National Crime Survey] crimes, there is a gray area of ambiguous events for which "victims" may be uncertain about what happened (e.g., whether an article was lost or stolen) or what was intended (e.g., whether a broken window was the result of vandalism or attempted burglary). . . . Especially as measured in a victimization survey, the presence of threat rests on victim interpretation of offender intent.

Meaning: the inherent difficulty of shared definitions

Providing a common frame of reference is not an easy task, and ensuring that respondents use it is tougher still. What the researcher offers the respondent as a frame of reference may not be one that the respondent commonly uses, and it may be difficult for the respondent to put on the researcher's angle of vision, like a pair of glasses with the wrong prescription. What "family" is to mean, for instance, may have to be specified lest respondents vary in their frame of reference from their immediate family to their far-flung extended family. (For that very reason, a researcher may abandon "family" entirely in favor of "people living in the household.") "The neighborhood" may also have just such an elastic character. Even if a researcher labors to define it ("we mean the houses in this block" or "the people living three blocks in every direction") the respondent may persist in thinking about the "neighborhood" however he or she always does. Whether these floating definitions really matter or not will depend on a lot of things—the construct, the research purposes, the population being sampled, the range of effective ambiguity—but one is not comfortable simply assuming across the board that these ambiguities *never* matter.

It is our impression that it used to be more common than it is now to arm interviewers with highly detailed definitions, such as "By 'family' we mean . . . " or "If the respondent asks how far the 'neighborhood' extends, say . . . . " It has been repeatedly pointed out by field supervisors that it is not interviewers who need to know the full definition of the question—it is respondents. Anything that an investigator wants respondents to hear or assume should be included in the question itself, so that *all* respondents will be exposed to it. We think this has been good counsel. We suspect, in any case, that these detailed instructions tucked into interviewer manuals are likely to be lost in the shuffle and the more of them there are, the worse it probably is. (We know of absolutely no research on this point.)

How one establishes clear definitions for shared meaning is not at all obvious in any general sense, nor is any general prescription likely. One simply has to keep on the lookout for any data or experience that may help, and one must keep trying to *gather* such data. For large-scale surveys, it seems inevitable that one will always be approximating, chipping away at ambiguity. If we are commonly reminded that our definitions are usually too vague or sloppy, it is also appropriate to remember that we can also err in expecting an unrealistic degree of exactness.

In a recent symposium on question wording, for example, the pursuit of the too-narrow was apparent. An experienced investigator reminded his peers that they must continue to get out into the field, themselves, lest they lose very valuable firsthand information; and he told of his own experience of ringing a doorbell at a home where the family watching television happened to be in full view. The person who proved to be his respondent was not in the livingroom when he rang the bell. She had gotten up and gone into the kitchen for a moment during the commercial, and came back into the livingroom just as he was ushered into the house. In the course of the interview, he asked her what she had been doing when the doorbell rang, and she said, "Watching television."

The point of the vignette was that for this particular study, which had to do with the watching of the *commercials*, when the woman went into the kitchen, she was no longer "watching television" from the investigator's standpoint (Webb, 1982: 63). From the woman's point of view, she was indeed watching—not every second, not without momentary deviations or interruptions, but watching nevertheless. The researchers wanted a more literal-minded account, but would they have been pleased to hear an account of this sort?

When the doorbell first rang, I was lifting my left foot and putting it ahead of my right foot. Or no, perhaps not. I rather think that I was lifting my right foot. . . . But when the doorbell *finished* ringing. . . . But I'm not really sure now. I may be mixing things up.

They probably wanted an account of mindful attention, not just eyes only, in any case. The respondent's very sensible "approximation" may well be the most precise estimate we can expect to get in the naturalistic setting of the household survey.

Recall of the past

If survey researchers were guided entirely by a concern for valid descriptive data, they would focus on *the current, the specific, the real* (Turner and Martin 1984, I: 299); it is increasingly apparent that memory questions in general tend to be difficult. Recalling an event or behavior can be especially difficult in any of several circumstances: if the decision was made almost mindlessly in the first place, if the event was so trivial that people have hardly given it a second thought since, if questions refer to events that happened long ago, or if they require the recall of many separate events. This is obvious enough, but some consumer surveys, for example, still ask a profusion of extremely detailed questions about the properties of a motor oil or a hair dye, and ask respondents to introspect intensively about why they bought one brand or another.

One is on safer ground asking about major life events that are likely to have been important or *salient* to the individual, but there is evidence that recall of even "important" events either fades with time, or requires specific cues to bring them into focus at the time of an interview. Hospitalizations, for instance, are presumably nontrivial events for most people, but recall of hospitalizations has been shown to erode with time (Cannell et al., 1979: 8). To enhance validity of the reporting of the past, five techniques have been recommended: (a) bounded recall, (b) narrowing of the reference period, (c) averaging, (d) landmarks, and (e) cueing. The first four address more directly the problem of dating events than the problem of remembering events at all. Only the fifth, cueing, tackles more directly the problem of forgetting the event itself. We shall consider each one briefly in turn.

Bounded recall addresses overreport due to "forward telescoping." There is quite good evidence that if one asks respondents about events in the last six months, they may actually see "beyond" that and include events that happened earlier (Neter and Waksberg, 1965), which of course creates overreporting. Bounded recall establishes a baseline measure in an initial survey. Then in a subsequent panel reinterview, one inquires about events that have happened since that first interview. This thoroughgoing strategy is of course available only to those with the resources to mount a panel study.

Sudman and his associates (1984), however, have recently used specific bounded recall periods in a single interview. For example, respondents were asked about health behavior in the previous calendar month and then were asked about the same events in the current calendar month. In an experimental design using this type of bounded recall, reports of illness were reduced by 7%-20%. The results were not compared to validation data, but they suggest a reduction in telescoping.

The effort in recent years to *narrow the reference period* for survey reporting is a welcome corrective, in general. Researchers probably used to require far too much, asking questions with an unexamined assumption that most people kept marvelously minute mental records of what and how much they ate, drank, walked, drove, bought, coughed, worried, or thought. As Turner and Martin (1984, I: 297) point out, long reference periods for measuring victimization are virtually "worthless if the answers are to be treated as factual." It is common now to reduce the reference period to six months or less. For certain events, at least, one can narrow the time period of interest to the very immediate past, such as last week, or yesterday. Rather than asking, "Do you get regular physical exercise? (IF YES), How many hours of physical exercise do you usually get in a week?" one can zero in on a narrow time period and ask, "Did you get any physical exercise yesterday?" And if yes, "How much?" By the time the study has been completed, that "yesterday" will sweep across several weeks, perhaps even months, and estimates will have to be analyzed with that range in mind, especially if the activity is one that varies seasonally. One may also want to determine whether or not this refers to "typical" or habitual experience.

One can correct for such variability by asking respondents to "*average.*" In research into college students, Schuman and his associates (1985: 958, 965) asked students about their time-use in a single day and a "typical" day in this sequence:

> The next few questions are about studying. First, apart from time spent in class, how much time, if any, did you study *yesterday*? By studying, we mean reading or any other assignment, writing, or review done outside of class.

Was that amount of time typical of the time you spent studying on *weekdays* during the past week or so?

(If No) What *was* the typical amount of time you spent studying on *weekdays* over the past week or so?

A similar sequence was then asked about week*ends*, because students' activities differ in the two periods. The investigators found that the "typical" or "averaging" question was more useful than the "single day" question because it took account of fluctuations in study time over the academic term.

The use of *landmarks* to aid dating is an experimental strategy that looks promising. Loftus and Marburger (1983) report positive results in experimental use of "landmark" events ("Since the eruption of Mt. St. Helens, has anyone beaten you up?") and major holidays such as New Year's Day to anchor the timing of other events. A similar technique using a calendar showing all major holidays of the year has been used as an aid in dating personal life events (DAS, 1985).

Providing *cues* to memory is still another strategy that is largely experimental. The purpose of cues is to stimulate recall by presenting a variety of associations. It recognizes the fact that because human memory uses a great variety of coding schemes to store information, what appears to be a "forgotten" event may be perfectly accessible if the correct storage file is tapped.

The victimization research that we have discussed set out specifically to stimulate recall of "crime" by describing concrete events. Instead of asking respondents if they had experienced "assaults," for instance, one item asked if anyone had used force against them "by grabbing, punching, choking, scratching, or biting." One purpose of this concreteness was to circumvent the premature aborting of memory search that is likely when a respondent has a (false) feeling of having nothing to report (Martin, 1986: 3-4). The cueing approach resulted in a 65% increase in victimization report, but the increase had to be discounted for events that were out of scope, events that happened before the six-month reference period, and other errors. The net increase, ranging from 19% to 39% (Martin, 1986: 64) is still impressive, but the results suggest that we cannot be entirely confident that more reporting is necessarily better reporting, as we often assume in assessing surveys of health, crime, and other kinds of behavioral data.

Results for both landmarks and cueing are not yet entirely clear or replicated extensively enough to suggest exactly how to activate memory most effectively, but the data on telescoping and forgetting continue to argue the need for new techniques.

Hypothetical questions

If we ask a hypothetical question, will we get a hypothetical answer— as some lighthearted critics have warned? Perhaps not, but the counsel of experience and research suggests that asking most people to imagine what if—what might have happened in their lives if things had been otherwise, or what they might do if—confronts them with a special task that is likely to be difficult. If the respondent is to take the mission seriously, it takes a good bit of imaginative projection as well as some time to mull over the possibilities. Certain survey objectives may cry for the use of hypothetical questions but it is well to be sure that it is a real necessity. When we ask hypothetical questions hoping to tap some underlying attitude, we know very little about what respondents actually have in mind when they answer. There appears to be only a little research on the point (Smith, 1981). It seems likely that respondents repair to their own personal experience when they have any, and yet if most people are trying to use their own experience, perhaps one can ask them about it directly.

There are instances in which hypothetical questions can nevertheless be valuable for certain research objectives. They usually represent an effort to *standardize* a stimulus because actual experiences range so widely, and the investigator does not know what set of experiences the respondent is bringing to the question. They can also be used in an effort to tie attitudes to some realistic contingencies. For example, people can be asked to imagine cost/benefit trade-offs. Would they favor such and such governmental program if it meant that their income tax would go up? Would they favor a tax cut if it meant that such and such service would go down? Would they favor X foreign policy if it meant that young men would be drafted in Y large numbers? And so on. Hypothetical questions provide no guarantee that respondents will feel the full force of political or economic realities, but they can try to add some realism to political rhetoric.

Hypothetical questions, nevertheless, are not easy and they deserve hard scrutiny before use. If one thinks that hypothetical questions are essential, ask them, but consider two other strategies as well: (1) Append to the battery on hypotheticals at least one question on actual experience, if possible; (2) more important, probe at least one of the hypotheticals for the respondent's frame of reference in answering the question. We are all in need of these kinds of data.

WIDESPREAD INFORMATION

Gallup's (1947: 687) early work on public information occasionally dramatized the widespread distribution of ignorance on certain topics. In the late 1940s, for example, Gallup Poll respondents were shown a map outlining the United States and asked to point to 10 of the best-known states (New York, California, Texas, and so on). That only 4% of Americans with a grade school education could locate all 10 states may not be surprising but those with at least some college education did not fare much better: only 8% could do so.

The finding that political information and interest are thinly distributed in some national groups has become a commonplace in research circles, but it was actually a discovery of survey research. Journalists and other educated observers who gathered their impressions from highly involved elites regularly exaggerated the knowledge and involvement of the broad public—and probably still do. Newcomers to survey research are also likely to assume that their own interests are mirrored in the general public. It can be very instructive to consult current poll and survey data on the broad public's level of information and interest.

When respondents know little about a subject, can one fill in some of the gaps on the spot? Investigators sometimes try, as in questions of this sort: "As you probably know, Honduras is right next to Nicaragua . . . " What the investigator presumably means is something like this:

> You probably don't really know this fact, or at least some people don't, or you may need reminding, so let me tell you that Honduras is right next to Nicaragua so that I can ask you the next question about military operations on the border between the two countries.

Most people probably cannot seize upon and use complex new information that quickly. The people who need instructions about where Honduras is are probably not entirely clear about where Nicaragua is, so the new information that these countries are neighbors may not be very illuminating, nor instant opinions on military implications very useful. As Nisbett et al. (1982) observe of experimental work with college students, "information is not necessarily informative."

Try it yourself. How ready are you with an opinion on this question, asked in a Harris survey in 1973:

I'd like to describe to you a new kind of insurance plan that would minimize the risk involved in investing in the stock market. You might want to read along with me on this card. (HAND RESPONDENT CARD "N.") According to this plan, you would be free to choose any stocks that you want to buy from an approved list of Blue Chip stocks like U.S. Steel, AT&T, or General Motors. An absolutely reliable company would guarantee to buy back the stock from you after ten years, but not earlier, for what you paid plus any gains in the value of the stock since you bought it. If the value of the stock decreased during the ten years you would still get back your original investment and the company, not you, would bear the loss. The price you would pay for this insurance against loss would be the dividends on the stock. This means that you would give up any dividends the stock would pay during the ten year period in exchange for this guarantee against loss.

If you wished to leave this insurance plan before the ten years were up, you would be free to do so and could sell the stock for the current market price. If the stock had increased in value, you would profit. If it declined, you would bear the loss, if you left the plan before the ten years were up. For leaving the plan, however, you would have to pay some charge like one or two years of dividends, which would vary according to how long you'd been in the plan. Remember, the firm offering this plan is absolutely reliable and the plan would be guaranteed by a major reputable insurance company. If such a plan were available, under which you would give up dividends on your stock in exchange for insurance against any loss on the money you put in, how interested would you be in participating in it—would you be definitely interested, do you think you might be interested but would like more information, do you think you would probably not be interested but would still like more information, or would you definitely not be interested at all [Harris, 1974]?

This question was asked not of stockbrokers or insurance agents but a national cross section. If respondents cannot be expected to learn complex new material in the course of a survey question, the example should suggest that some survey questions are—impossible.

Some Interesting Complexities

The counsel to simplicity neglects three interesting, more complex approaches to question design. We will discuss them here briefly not because either experience or general research strategy gives us much guidance into their application but because their use raises important questions. We will consider, in turn, factorial design (using vignettes), ranking scales, and magnitude estimation scales.

Factorial surveys use vignettes or "stories" in the study of judgment, decision-making, or attribution processes. The vignette itself is not new to survey research, but its design and randomization by computer program is. The following example is adapted from Alexander and Becker (1978: 94):

> Mr. Miller is a salesman who works for you. He comes into your office one morning to tell you that he has been drinking on the job. Miller is white, about 22, has been working for you for three months, and shows an average performance record.

The vignette factors are then varied—Mr. Miller becomes a Ms., age 56, black, an employee of 20 years, with an outstanding work record, and her drinking on the job has been observed by a trusted coworker. Respondents are asked to explain how they feel about each concrete instance.

When we vary dichotomies on even six variables, as in this example (sex, age, race, length of employment, work performance record, and source of information), 64 (2 to the 6th power) possible vignette combinations result—and many more factors would be of interest as well. The question-writing chores for such factorial designs begin to look rather daunting. Computer programs are designed not only to reduce these mechanical labors but also to randomize the combinations of factors and reduce these combinations to those of greatest analytic interest (Alexander and Becker, 1978: 96).

Factorial surveys have some very attractive features. To respondents, vignettes offer concrete, detailed situations on which to make judgments rather than the demand for abstract generalizations. Even though the questions are hypothetical, vignettes reduce the need for respondents to be insightful and conscious of their own thought processes. And one can construct vignettes to disentangle multicollinearity of the real world, where, for example, more expensive houses will also tend to be the larger houses, in better repair, located on more attractive lots, and so forth (Rossi and Anderson, 1982: 22).

Much of the early work in factorial surveys has been conducted with special samples, such as specific occupational groups and college students, but two 1986 surveys will be of special interest because they use factorial survey design with samples of the general public: the metropolitan cross-section of the Detroit Area Study, and the national cross-section of the General Social Survey of the National Opinion Research Center. Two features are common to both surveys. The number of vignettes is limited (to 15 in one case; to two groups of 10 in the other) on the basis of pretest evidence that beyond this number respondents tended to become fatigued or bored. These vignettes are also presented as self-administered sections in a survey that is otherwise face-to-face. This has the advantage of being less monotonous in delivery than oral pretest presentation seemed to be, but it has the counterpart disadvantage that interviewers cannot assess the degree of respondents' comprehension, or probe for ambiguity, or offer clarification. (Mellinger et al., 1982, used oral presentation in their vignette study of risk-benefit dilemmas in biomedical research and concluded that respondents' comprehension was adequate to the complex task.)

Methodological work is not yet widely available on various important issues. How does the task difficulty of vignettes compare with that of other survey questions? How do respondents view the task? How much of the information, which is rather densely packed into these vignettes, is actually absorbed by the respondent? (How much of the information is indeed "informative"?) What is the practical limit on the number of factors that can be varied? Are there context effects of the kind that we sometimes observe in traditional survey questions? Or effects from the order of presentation of the story elements? (See Chapter 2.) This is a tall order for research findings, which we cannot fill even for many, more conventional approaches to survey measurement, so it is hardly surprising that newer techniques such as factorial surveys have not yet inspired much of this kind of investigation. But the lack should make for caution, for we do not know much yet about how factorial surveys behave.

Ranking scales have a longer history in survey research. In the early 1920s, as distinguished an experimental psychologist/ market researcher as Daniel Starch (1923: 197) presented respondents with ranking scales that now look towering. For example:

What do you consider the most important in buying boys' and children's clothing:

Material	Comfort
Durability	"Wear like iron"
Union made	Price

Style	Reputation of the firm
Tailoring	Fit
"Satisfaction or money back" guarantee	Maker's guarantee
	Merchant's guarantee

And Starch asked respondents to rank all 13 items in the order of importance.

Tasks of this scope were soon seen to be much too difficult (Franzen, 1936: 6) and in our own time, rank orders of this size are all but invisible in the literature. Shorter rankings are not uncommon—lists of four or five, for example—as well as partial rank orders such as Kohn's list of qualities desirable in children. Kohn (1969) also presents respondents with thirteen items, as it happens, in the question we have already noted:

- that a child have good manners
- tries hard to succeed
- is interested in how and why things happen, etc.

But respondents are given the simpler task of choosing, first, the three most desirable qualities and then one of that set that is most desirable of all. (They are also asked the same selection sequence for the least desirable qualities.) Kohn has used the ranked measures in an influential study of parental values, in which bipolar values of self-direction and conformity are found to be associated with higher and lower occupational status, respectively. It is widely agreed that rankings, even of this modified form, are more difficult than rating scales. The latter do not require choices among items; they take less time; and they can also be administered readily over the telephone in a way that long rank orders cannot, for they usually require "show cards." Ranking, nevertheless, is not without advantages. Among other things, the very fact that ranks are more difficult may help elicit the appropriate effort from respondents. It is worth asking, nevertheless, whether or not ranking is easy *enough* to be used in cross-section samples and whether or not results from it are comparable to those from rating scales.

Alwin and Krosnick's (1985) split sample experiments deal with these issues. First, they find that the relative importance given the qualities is very similar with rankings and ratings. Both measures also show the same "latent" dimensions, self-direction, and conformity. But they do *not* show the same relationships to predictor variables. Self-direction is positively correlated with education and income when rankings are used but not when ratings are used. As Alwin and Krosnick observe, the ranking technique may force a contrast between self-direction and conformity by asking respondents to make choices that they may not otherwise make. Ranks may measure not only the latent dimension of contrast between self-direction and conformity but also the very "ability to see logical contrast in the list of ranked qualities" (Alwin and Krosnick, 1985: 549).

This finding raises a very basic issue. When we ask questions that are widely acknowledged to be difficult ones, such as rank ordering, how are we to interpret observed relationships to education? Is this a "real-world" finding, or one that is compromised by artifactual properties because the highly educated bring something special to the task itself? Or should an artifact of this sort be considered a social fact? *Ratings* are not without their problems too, and indeed Krosnick and Alwin (forthcoming), in further work, conclude that, on balance, rankings still have more to recommend them for the study of values than ratings do. But these findings and their recent evidence of primacy and recency effects in the administrations of the Kohn lists suggest that we need much more guidance from research to understand question effects from the use of ranking scales.

Magnitude estimation scales are a third, more complex, technique of interest. They represent contemporary efforts to adapt to the measurement of social opinion the kinds of ratio scales developed in psychophysical measurement. Some social scientists have been drawn to this kind of scaling in frustration at the limits posed by the ordinal measurement of so much survey work: the loss of information when categories arbitrarily constrain the range of opinion; and the loss of precision in applying to ordinal measurement statistics appropriate to interval levels of measurement. Magnitude scaling of attitudes has been "calibrated" through numeric estimation and physical line-length estimation of physical stimuli such as light and sound.

The application of numeric estimation to social opinions is shown in this example (Lodge, 1981: 19):

> I would like to ask your opinion about how serious YOU think certain crimes are. The first situation is, "A person steals a bicycle parked on the street." This has been given a score of 10 to show its seriousness. Use this situation to judge all others. For example, if you think a situation is 20 TIMES MORE serious than the bicycle

theft, the number you tell me should be around 200, or if you think it is HALF AS SERIOUS, the number you tell me should be around 5, and so on. . . .
COMPARED TO THE BICYCLE THEFT AT SCORE 10, HOW SERIOUS IS:
A parent beats his young child with his fists. The child requires hospitalization.
A person plants a bomb in a public building. The bomb explodes and 20 people are killed . . .

And so on.
In "line production," respondents are asked to draw lines that correspond to ratio judgments of the same kind, as in this example:

Some people believe that we should spend much less money for defense. Others feel that defense should be increased. And, of course, some other people have opinions in between.

Compared to the government's present level of defense spending, do you think we should increase defense spending, keep it about the same as now, or decrease defense spending [Lodge, 1981: 63]?

Then respondents are asked to draw a reference line to show what the government is currently spending on defense, and then to draw a response line to indicate how much the respondent favors an increase or decrease in defense spending. (In this use, the line is intended to represent a measure of intensity with which respondents hold their opinions, not the amount of increase or decrease in spending that they want.)
Magnitude scaling has shown some interesting results. Lodge (1981: 77) reports work showing an increase of 12%-15% in variance explained from the use of magnitude over ordinal scaling. In more recent work, Norpoth and Lodge (1985) report the successful use of magnitude scaling in a study of sophistication and intellectual structure of political attitudes. But the technique also poses some special problems. For instance, respondents must be given instruction and practice in making proportional judgment so that investigators can be sure that respondents have the competence to do so and are not reverting in their social opinion scales to the ordinal judgments so commonly used in surveys. Can people handle the tasks of numeric estimation—if, as we have been warned in other studies, many people shy away from such numeric tasks as calculating proportions? Are there any special precautions that

we might take to make use of the interesting properties of these measures without incurring unduly heavy tasks for the respondent or unacceptable losses of information? We have little information about such questions. There has been little methodological work into magnitude scaling, perhaps because there are some special costs and burdens in undertaking the design at all.

Although these more complex techniques have considerable interest and potential usefulness in survey research, there is much about them that we do not yet understand. We are better guided, for now, by the counsel of experience or general research strategy that we have reviewed in this chapter, and by the findings of experiment, to which we now turn in Chapter 2.

2. THE EXPERIMENTAL EVIDENCE

Informal knowledge and personal experience have played a larger role in the design of survey questions than formal results from split sample experiments, probably because the implications for practice from such experiments are not always clear. Yet, important practical guidance can be drawn from experimental findings, especially those of the last decade or so. In this chapter we begin with some specific implications from the research literature and then turn to a number of general lessons.

Specific Questions
Are Better Than General Ones

The goal of standardized measurement is central to survey research. For the reasons we have noted, it has been considered essential to keep the wording of questions constant across respondents. But, of course, even the same question sometimes means different things to different people. Recent research indicates that this is particularly likely with general questions. The more general the question, the wider the range of interpretations it may be given. By contrast, wording that is specific and concrete is more apt to communicate uniform meaning.

The advantages of specificity can be seen in an experiment carried out by Belson and Duncan (1962) on British newspaper and magazine readership. A question that presented respondents with a list of periodicals and asked them to check those they had looked at the previous day was compared with one that asked respondents simply to list the newspapers and magazines they had looked at the previous day.

The most striking difference between forms was in the proportion mentioning *Radio Times*, a publication similar to the American *TV Guide*. More than five times as many people mentioned it on the checklist as on the other form (38% versus 7%). Apparently, some people thought of *Radio Times* as a magazine, but others did not. On the version where periodical titles were not mentioned, these different understandings affected people's answers. On the checklist, this extraneous source of variation was avoided, and a more consistent measurement across respondents was obtained.

The Belson and Duncan study also points to a second advantage of specificity. In addition to more precise communication of question intent, specificity aids respondent recall. Although the *Radio Times* difference was far and away the largest, the checklist produced higher readership estimates for every publication. Unaided, respondents had difficulty recalling all the magazines and newspapers they looked at yesterday. Seeing a list of possibilities helped them remember. (The lack of validation data means we cannot definitively rule out the possibility that people exaggerated their reading on the checklist, yet the pattern of results makes this unlikely. For example, the form differences were much smaller for newspapers than for magazines, as one would expect given that newspaper reading is a daily activity and thus easier to recall than less regular magazine reading.)

The virtues of specificity are by no means limited to items about behavior. A series of experiments on the measurement of happiness demonstrates the same point for attitude questions (Turner, 1984). The experiments varied the order in which these two questions were asked:

- Taken altogether, how would you say things are these days: would you say that you are very happy, pretty happy or not too happy?
- Taking all things together, how would you describe your marriage: would you say that your marriage is very happy, pretty happy or not too happy?

The first question is very general. It asks about unspecified "things." People may answer in terms of different combinations of their health, job, marriage, and so on. This probably explains why answers to the general question are affected by whether it is asked before or after the marital happiness question. Either of two processes may occur: When the marriage question is asked first, respondents' feelings about their marriage may suffuse their judgment about life in general; alternatively, answering the marriage question first may lead respondents to subtract that topic from the second question bearing on things in general.

The specific question on marital happiness, on the other hand, is not vulnerable to this order effect. Respondents answer the marital happiness question the same way, regardless of whether it comes before or after the general happiness question (Turner, 1984). Its greater specificity apparently makes its interpretation less subject to influence from factors like question placement. It is the meaning of more abstract, less definite items that are particularly prone to such problems (Kalton et al., 1978; Smith, 1981).

One further disadvantage of general items is worth mentioning. Responses to general attitude items are poorer predictors of behavior than responses to specific attitude questions. Indeed, the more specific an attitude item, the stronger the connection between attitudes and behavior. Thus, for example, an attitude question about open housing laws was a better predictor of willingness to sign petitions about the issue than a series of questions measuring general racial prejudice (Brannon et al., 1973).

Despite this catalogue of weaknesses, general questions cannot be ruled out entirely. They have their uses when a "global" measure is of analytic interest; when there is not the time or space to ask about *everything* in specific detail; and when the comparison of general and specific views is itself of interest.

When to Leave It Open and When to Close It

A widespread criticism of closed questions is that they force people to choose among offered alternatives instead of answering in their own words. Yet precisely because closed questions spell out the response options, they are more specific than open questions, and therefore more apt to communicate the same frame of reference to all respondents.

This advantage of the closed form is demonstrated in the results of an experiment on work values that compared the following two questions (Schuman and Presser, 1981):

People look for different things in a job. What would you most prefer in a job?

People look for different things in a job. Which one of the following five things would you most prefer in a job—work that pays well; work that gives a feeling of accomplishment; work where there is not too much supervision and you make most decisions yourself; work that is pleasant and where the other people are nice to work with; or work that is steady with little chance of being laid off?

On the open form, many respondents said "the pay" was the most important aspect of a job. There was evidence that some of these individuals meant "high pay" whereas others meant "steady pay." But both kinds of answers were expressed in the same words, making it impossible to separate the two. The closed form solved this problem. Individuals of the first sort chose "work that pays well," whereas those of the second type chose "work that is steady." Thus building distinctions into the answer categories can more accurately tap differences among respondents than letting people answer in their own words.

Of course, this will only be true if the response categories have been appropriately designed. In another open-closed experiment, people were asked what they thought was the most important problem facing the nation (Schuman and Presser, 1981: 86). As the survey began, the U.S. was hit with an unexpected natural-gas shortage. This was reflected on the open version, where 22% said the "energy shortage" was the most important problem. On the closed version, designed without knowledge of the energy problem, there was hardly a trace of concern about the shortage, over 99% choosing one of the five offered alternatives (unemployment, crime, inflation, leadership quality, and breakdown of morals and religion). Thus when not enough is known to write appropriate response categories, open questions are to be preferred.

A second area in which open questions have been shown to be better than closed ones is the measurement of sensitive or disapproved behavior. Bradburn and Sudman (1979) compared open and closed estimates of drinking and sexual activity, both of which are known to be underreported in surveys. The closed questions had the response categories, "never, once a year or less, every few months, once a month, every few weeks, once a week, several times a week, and daily," The open questions, of course, had no response categories. In every case (beer, wine, liquor, petting, intercourse, and masturbation), reported frequencies were significantly higher on the open form. Apparently, the presence of the low-frequency categories on the closed form makes people less willing to admit to higher frequencies.

There are other special purposes for which open questions are better suited than closed items (to measure salience, for example, or to capture modes of expression). But in most instances, a carefully pretested closed form is to be preferred for its greater specificity.

Offer a No Opinion Option

The typical survey question incorporates assumptions not only about the nature of what is to be measured, but also about its very existence. "The trouble is," as Katz (1940: 282) perceived early in the development of public opinion measurement, "that the polls have often assumed that because a problem is of practical importance or of political interest, therefore there is a public opinion on the problem which can be measured."

This problem is intensified by the standard survey practice of not including "don't know" or "no opinion" as a response option mentioned in the question. Experimental research shows that many more people will say "don't know" when that alternative is explicitly offered than when it is not. Such filtering for no opinion generally affects from about an eighth to a third of those interviewed (Bishop et al., 1980a; Schuman and Presser, 1981).

The size of the effect is partly a function of the way in which the don't know option is offered. Making the filter a separate question (example A) has a larger effect than simply including "no opinion" as one of the response options (example B).

- (A) Here is a statement about another country. Not everyone has an opinion on this. If you do not have an opinion just say so. Here's the statement: The Russian leaders are basically trying to get along with America. Do you have an opinion on that? (IF YES:) Do you agree or disagree?
- (B) Here is a statement about another country. The Russian leaders are basically trying to get along with America. Do you agree, disagree, or do you not have an opinion on that?

Likewise, "Have you thought much about this issue?" is a stronger filter than "Do you have an opinion on this?" (Schuman and Presser, 1981).

Even when asked *un*filtered questions, however, most survey respondents do not mindlessly give opinions when they do not have them. About 70% of American adults volunteer "don't know" to unfiltered items about plausible sounding but obscure or fictitious issues (Bishop et al., 1980b; Schuman and Presser, 1981). On the other hand, some respondents apparently do manufacture opinions on the spot, and thus filtering for "don't know" is a good practice.

Filtering is especially important toward the beginning of an interview to make clear to respondents that no opinion is a legitimate answer. Doing so at the outset, as well as training interviewers to accept "don't knows," should also reduce the need—and monotony—of filtering routinely throughout an interview.

Omit the Middle Alternative and Measure Intensity

Survey researchers disagree about whether or not middle alternatives should be included in the wording of questions. Moser and Kalton (1972: 344) argue that "there is clearly a risk in suggesting a noncommittal answer to the respondent." Yet as early as 1944, Rugg and Cantril (1944: 33) argued for offering the middle alternative "in that it provides for an additional graduation of opinion."

Split sample experiments indicate that the resolution of the issue is important, as results depend on whether or not the middle ground is provided. It is not unusual for 20% of those interviewed to *choose* a middle alternative when it is offered although they would not *volunteer* it if it were not mentioned. Strikingly, however, this tends to have a limited impact on the distribution of responses in other categories. This is illustrated in various experiments carried out by Schuman and Presser (1981). For example:

Should divorce in this country be easier or more difficult to obtain than it is now?		Should divorce in this country be easier to obtain, more difficult to obtain, or stay as it is now?	
Easier	28.9	Easier	22.7
More difficult	44.5	More difficult	32.7
Stay as is (volunteered)	21.7	Stay as is	40.2
Don't know	4.9	Don't know	4.3
Total	100.0%	Total	100.0%

Although the size of the middle category is very different on the two forms, the ratio of "easier" to "more difficult" is essentially unaffected by form. Holding aside the middle answers and the don't knows, about 40% say "easier" and 60% "more difficult" on both forms.

Who, then, are the respondents affected by the presence of a middle category? Intensity is the major characteristic that distinguishes them from those who give the same answer regardless of question wording. Offering a middle position makes less difference to individuals who feel strongly about an issue than it does to those who do not feel strongly.

These results suggest a solution to the middle alternative wording problem. Do not explicitly provide the middle category, and thereby avoid losing information about the direction in which some people lean, but follow the question with an intensity item, thus separating those who definitely occupy a position from those who only lean toward it.

How to Measure Intensity

The measurement of intensity is useful not only as a follow-up for items with logical middle positions, but for attitude questions generally. Strength of feeling has been shown to predict both attitude stability and attitude constraint. Thus strength measures can identify respondents who will be more consistent over time as well as more consistent between topics (Schuman and Presser, 1981; Smith, 1983).

Asking questions about intensity or centrality may also enhance our understanding of the nature of public opinion on an issue. In the late 1970s, for example, Americans were fairly evenly split in response to a question about whether or not a married woman should have access to a legal abortion, but this distribution concealed very different strengths of feeling on the two sides. Opponents of abortion were six times more likely than "pro-choice" advocates to say that they felt extremely strongly about the issue (Schuman and Presser, 1981: 246). Without the strength of feeling data, an analyst would have been more apt to misinterpret the even split between abortion proponents and opponents. (The so-called "mushiness index" is another way of getting at this dimension of public opinion; see *Public Opinion*, 1981.)

Two of the most commonly used intensity indicators are "strongly agree, agree, disagree, or strongly disagree" items (example A) and seven-point scales labeled at either end by opposing positions (example B).

(A) Now I'm going to read several statements. Please tell me whether you strongly agree, agree, disagree, or strongly disagree with each. "It is much better for everyone involved if the man is the achiever outside the home and the woman takes care of the home and the family." Do you strongly agree, agree, disagree, or strongly disagree?

(B) Some people feel the federal government should take action to reduce the inflation rate even if it means that unemployment would go up a lot. Others feel the government should take action to reduce the rate of unemployment even if it means that inflation would go up a lot. Where would you place yourself on this scale?
Reduce Inflation   1 2 3 4 5 6 7   Reduce Unemployment

These approaches confound extremity, a dimension of attitudinal position, with intensity, how strongly a position is felt. Although intensity and extremity may frequently covary, individuals may hold an extreme position with little feeling, or invest a middle of the road position with considerable passion. Without separate questions for position and intensity (e.g., following a question about direction of opinion with an item like "How strongly do you feel about that—extremely strongly, very strongly, somewhat strongly, or not at all strongly?"), it is not possible to disentangle these dimensions.

Use Forced-Choice Questions, Not Agree-Disagree Statements

One of the most popular forms of attitude measurement is the agree-disagree statement. It is also the form that has come under most attack by methodologists. The approach suffers from "acquiescence response set"—the tendency of respondents to agree irrespective of item content. Consider this pair of items:

It is hardly fair to bring children into the world, the way things look for the future.

Children born today have a wonderful future to look forward to.

Although these items seem completely contradictory, Lenski and Leggett (1960) report that about a tenth of their sample agreed to both, a finding echoed in the results of split sample experiments.

Moreover, acquiescing is related to education. Its incidence is greatest among individuals who have had little schooling. Consequently, the use of agree-disagree items may distort conclusions about the relationship between education and opinion, as in the following example (Schuman and Presser, 1981: 223):

	Years of Schooling		
	0-11	12	13+
Would you say that most men are better suited emotionally for politics than are most women, that men and women are equally suited, or that women are better suited than men in this area?			
Percent "men better suited"	33	38	28
Do you agree or disagree with this statement: Most men are better suited emotionally for politics than are most women.			
Percent "agree"	57	44	39

The forced-choice form of this item shows that there is essentially no relationship between education and opinion about women in politics. (The difference between groups does not exceed sampling error.) On the agree-disagree version, by contrast, there is a clear relationship, less-educated respondents being more likely to give the traditional answer. But this is due to the greater tendency of the less educated to acquiesce, not to a real difference in attitudes toward women.

More generally, forced-choice items are more apt to encourage a considered response than are agree-disagree statements. Taken by itself, "The government should see to it that everyone receives adequate medical care," may have a plausible ring to it. Asked alone, "Everyone should be responsible for their own medical care," also may seem sensible. Thus for most purposes, the better survey item is, "Should the government see to it that everyone receives adequate medical care, or should everyone be responsible for their own medical care?"

The Problem of Question Order

Survey respondents are sensitive to the context in which a question is asked, as well as to the particular words used to ask it. As a result, the meaning of almost any question can be altered by a preceding question. Consider the item, "In general, do you think the courts in this area deal too harshly or not harshly enough with criminals?" In most contexts, respondents will interpret "this area" to mean a geographical location. Yet a very different meaning can be conveyed by asking the question in this context:

- Do you think the United States should forbid public speeches in favor of Communism?
- In general, do you think the courts in this area deal too harshly or not harshly enough with criminals?

In a pretest using this sequence, some respondents thought that the courts item referred to judicial treatment of public speeches advocating communism.

As a general rule, however, items affect one another mainly when their content is clearly related, as in the marriage and general happiness example discussed earlier (where one object subsumes the other), or when the answer to one question has an obvious implication for the answer to another. Thus fewer people say their taxes are too high after being asked a series of items about whether government spending should be increased in various areas (Turner and Krauss, 1978). Similarly, more people say America should let Soviet journalists into the U.S. if they have just been asked if the Soviet Union should admit American journalists (Hyman and Sheatsley, 1950).

In each of these examples, some respondents bring their answers to an item into line with what they have said to another item. One way to think about this is in terms of consistency. Another way of looking at it is in terms of salience. Earlier questions may make some experiences or judgments more salient or available to the respondent than they otherwise would be. This appears to have happened in an experiment on measuring crime (Cowan et al., 1978). A questionnaire that asked only factual items about whether the respondent had been criminally victimized in the last twelve months was compared with one that was prefaced by a series of attitude items about crime. People reported significantly more crime on the version preceded by the attitude questions. Answering the attitude items apparently stimulated memories of actual criminal events, although it is of interest to note that the differences occurred mainly for the more frequent, less serious kinds of crime.

Notwithstanding these examples, it should be emphasized that numerous experiments with related questions show no context effect. Thus, to take one instance, evaluations of President Nixon's job performance were unaffected by whether they followed a question about his possible impeachment (Hitlin, 1976). Many similar instances of order having no effect may be found in Schuman and Presser (1981).

Unlike the wording decisions we have reviewed, however, there are almost no experimentally based general rules to order questions. Before there was systematic study of the matter, experienced researchers recommended that general questions be asked *before* specific ones, in a "funnel" sequence (Kahn and Cannell, 1957). The research we reviewed earlier on general and specific items supports this intuition. Otherwise, in the case of attitudes, even where context is shown to have an effect, it is frequently unclear that one order is better than another. Instead, each order may reveal a different facet of the issue being studied.

Wording Effects:
Potentially Important But Unpredictable

The most basic finding from research on question wording is a double edged one: Even small changes in wording can shift the answers of many respondents, but it is frequently difficult to predict in advance whether or not a wording change will have such an effect. "Forbid" and "allow," for example, are logical opposites, and thus substituting one for the other in the question "Do you think the United States should [allow/forbid] public speeches against democracy?" might easily be assumed to have no effect. Yet it turns out that many more people are willing to "not allow" such speeches than are willing to "forbid" them. On the other hand, referring to something as "bad and dangerous" would seem to load a question and thus have a noticeable impact on respondents. In fact, the following two items yielded identical results:

- There are some people who are against all churches and religion. If such a person wanted to make a speech in your (city/town/community) against churches and religion, should he be allowed to speak, or not?

- There are always some people whose ideas are considered bad or dangerous by other people. For instance, somebody who is against all churches and religion. If such a person wanted to make a speech in your (city/town/community) against churches and religion, should he be allowed to speak, or not?

About two-thirds of American adults were in favor of free speech on both forms (Schuman and Presser, 1981: 289-290).

Similar results are not uncommon. Consider this pair of examples from experiments conducted at the outset of the Second World War (Rugg and Cantril, 1944: 44):

(A) Do you think the United States will go into the war before it is over?

Yes 41%   No 33%   Don't Know 26%

(B) Do you think the United States will succeed in staying out of the war?

Yes 44%   No 30%   Don't Know 26%

Despite the apparently trivial change in wording, respondents were clearly affected. In the following pair of questions, however, there is a substantial change in wording without any effect at all.

(A) Some people say that since Germany is now fighting Russia, as well as Britain, it is not as necessary for this country to help Britain. Do you agree or disagree with this?

Agree 20%   Disagree 72%   No Opinion 8%

(B) Some people say that since Germany will probably defeat Russia within a few weeks and then turn her full strength against Britain, it is more important than ever that we help Britain. Do you agree or disagree with this?

Agree 71%   Disagree 19%   No Opinion 10%

Results like these demonstrate the subtleties and complexities inherent in language. They show that respondents tend to be constrained by the exact words of a question—as well they should be. (If we got the same answers no matter what wording we used, survey research would have no scientific basis at all.) Such results also indicate the importance of not basing conclusions on results from a single question. In this regard, four approaches deserve wider use.

CREATE SPLIT SAMPLE COMPARISONS

Wording experiments need not be confined to methodological research, but can be built into all surveys, at least for some items. Experiments of modest scope can be purchased at a minor increase in clerical costs. Multiple questionnaires are not needed, as one can simply construct a set of skip patterns for the different question wordings, and establish a random procedure by which the interviewer is directed to one or the other. This is a very easy matter with Computer Assisted Telephone Interviewing but even without the computer it may be straightforwardly accomplished by a procedure in which every other listing, after a random start, is designated A or B, leaving nothing to interviewer choice.

The risk accompanying wording experiments is learning that two forms of the "same" question are not equivalent. This reduces the sample size, as one would no longer be justified in combining these experimental apples and oranges in the analysis. If the experiment turned on a central question, this could be a sore loss. From a scientific perspective, of course, it might be a sorer loss if one *failed* to uncover these qualifications, ambiguities, or differences.

USE OPEN FOLLOW-UPS TO CLOSED QUESTIONS

Probes of closed questions provide another window on the meaning of items and an efficient way of combining some advantages of both open and closed questions. In the 1983 Detroit Area Study of attitudes and experiences regarding welfare, for example, a substantial majority endorsed the proposition that "Government is trying to do too many things that should be left to individuals and private businesses." Of the sample, 72% agreed that the government had taken on too many functions—at least this is what the investigators had meant by the question. When agreeing respondents were asked the follow-up question, "What things do you feel should be left to individuals or private businesses?" over a quarter could not answer at all. They could not think of anything "offhand" or "didn't know." Others said "Taxes are too high" or inveighed vaguely against government ("Government shouldn't be messing into things all the time—I'm for freedom"). Probing for the respondent's meaning revealed the flaws of what may have been an overly intellectual question. Thus the answers to open follow-ups can provide valuable guidance in the analysis of closed questions.

USE RANDOM PROBES

One can invest the time available for probing a few key questions and ask them of everyone. Or one can ask probes contingently of a subset of people who respond in certain ways, as in the case of those who agreed to the antigovernment item. Another approach is to spread a net of follow-up questions more thinly and widely, asking each respondent a small number of probes distributed randomly over the entire questionnaire.

In Schuman's design (1966) the interviewer probes nondirectively after the respondent has selected an alternative to a closed question, in wording of this sort:

- Could you tell me a little more about what you mean?
- Could you say more about what you have in mind?
- I see—could you give me an example?

The interviewer does not select the questions to be probed; rather, the questions are selected in advance of the interview by a random procedure, and marked on the questionnaire.

The random probe can be used extensively to provide a sample of follow-up answers for an entire questionnaire or more selectively for a subset of questions. Either way, it is valuable for three purposes: First, to pinpoint items that were particularly troublesome for respondents; second, to identify respondents whose understanding of the questionnaire was imperfect enough that they probably contributed mainly error to the study; and third, as a qualitative aid to interpretation.

This last use is illustrated in a study of black attitudes conducted by Schuman and Hatchett (1974). In analyzing the item "Generally speaking, do you feel (blacks/Negroes) have more, less, or the same duty as whites to obey the law?" it was expected that those who answered "less" would show higher than average scores on alienation. They did, but curiously, so did those who said blacks had "more" duty to be law-abiding.

Responses from the random probe indicated that this latter group interpreted the question in terms of blacks' greater need (rather than "duty") to be law-abiding because of racial discrimination:

- Whites can get away with things Negroes can't.
- Negroes have to be more careful.

In this context, the higher alienation scores for respondents who believed blacks had more duty to be law-abiding were not surprising.

ASK MULTIPLE QUESTIONS ON A TOPIC

The knowledge that any one survey item may be beset by a host of extraneous influences unique to it has led survey researchers to scale or index construction. It is probably fair to say, however, that the faith that scales can overcome the defects of single questions is not as strong as it once was. For one reason, scales can actually compound wording or form effects. If agree-disagree items, for instance, are prey to acquiescence, a battery of such items will amplify the distortion.

For another reason, scales may be bent out of shape by change over time. Items that correlate highly with each other at one point may move in different directions over time, as in this example from the National Election Study. As the graph shows (see next page), 3 of the 4 measures moved together quite nicely, rising in the 1950s and declining in the 1960s, suggesting that they each tapped some general facet of political efficacy. The fourth item, however, went its own way, rising consistently across the tide. Philip Converse (1972) interprets this as a response to the political activity of the 1960s, which featured not only voting but demonstrations, marches, and so on. More to our purposes here, he draws a methodological moral (p. 329):

> This is an interesting case . . . of a scale deemed unidimensional by Guttman criteria in 1952, one component of which has pulled out of line rather markedly in response to phenotypic events in a subsequent period. Our analysis of these trends would have been greatly muddied if we had proceeded with the composite scale taken as a whole.

So there is no real reprieve. Investigators wisely seek multiple and scaled measures but there is no guarantee they will remain scales. They may be scattered by the winds of change into component or single items that require individual interpretation. Yet single questions survive, too, for the simple reason that one can never, in a single survey, incorporate multiple measures of *everything*.

Multiple measures are nevertheless the strategy of choice. Relying on single questions makes it difficult to uncover complexity. Using multiple indicators makes it easier to discover where or how our understanding of the world is inadequate. The study of political party identification is an instructive case in point. For decades, party identification was seen by political scientists as simply the sense of attachment felt toward one of the parties, and was measured as follows:

- Generally speaking, do you usually think of yourself as a Republican, a Democrat, an Independent, or what?

- IF REPUBLICAN OR DEMOCRAT: Would you call yourself a strong (Republican/Democrat) or a not very strong (Republican/Democrat)?
- IF INDEPENDENT: Do you think of yourself as closer to the Republican or Democratic Party?

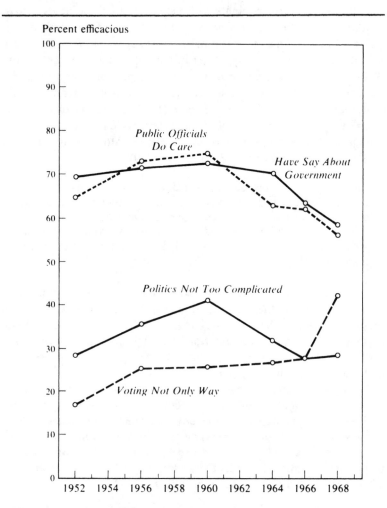

Percent efficacious

NOTE: From "Human Meaning of Social Change," edited by Angus Campbell and Philip Converse. Copyright © 1972 by the Russell Sage Foundation. Reprinted by permission of Basic Books, Inc., Publisher.

Figure 1: Trends in Responses to Political Efficacy Items, 1952-1968

This measurement approach assumes that people can identify with only one party and that political independence is nothing more than the absence of identification with a party. Recent research suggests that these assumptions are unjustified. In an analysis of 1980 national data, for example, Weisberg (1980) reports that a fifth of those classified as strong partisans by the traditional measure thought of themselves as Independents *as well as* party supporters. Results like these are leading to a reconceptualization of party identification as involving separate attitudes toward at least four objects: political parties in general, the Republican party, the Democratic party, and political independence. Thus to quote Weisberg (1980):

> Some people might be Independents because they dislike both parties, while others might be Independents because they like both parties equally, and still others might be Independents because they positively value political independence. Indeed, some people might consider themselves both Republicans (or Democrats) and Independents, particularly if they generally support Republican issue stands but feel that one should vote on the basis of issues rather than party labels.

Many if not most of the issues asked about in surveys are as complex as party identification. Consider, for instance, the debate about gun control. When Americans are asked if they favor banning private ownership of guns, a large majority expresses opposition. By contrast, when they are asked if they favor a law requiring a police permit before purchasing a gun, an equally large majority expresses support (Wright, 1981). These results reveal some of the complexity of attitudes toward this issue. Americans favor certain forms of gun control and oppose others. Asking multiple items not only facilitates the discovery of these contingencies and qualifications but makes the analyst less likely to fall into the trap of reporting a single number as representing public opinion on an issue.

As a general strategy, therefore, one should look for questions that cast light at different angles. In using multiple measures of this sort, we are not aspiring to experiment. Rather, we are trying to escape the confines of any single question to a richer context of inquiry—the prime objective of the two kinds of counsel we have so far considered, the lore of experience and the evidence of systematic experiment, as well as that of the one to which we turn in the next chapter, the continuous exploration of pretesting.

3. THE TOOLS AT HAND

Every questionnaire must, finally, be handcrafted. It is not only that questionnaire writing must be "artful"; each questionnaire is also unique, an original. A designer must cut and try, see how it looks and sounds, see how people react to it, and then cut again, and try again. Handcrafting a questionnaire involves successive trials, which we shall consider here in two stages: exploration and pretesting.

Exploration

The crafting of a questionnaire involves intellectual preparation of all sorts, well prior to the exploration we consider here. One must have a clear set of research purposes, knowledge of work on the problem that has already been conducted ("the literature" bearing on concepts and data), and some lively notions of how a survey could shed some new light. How should one start on the preliminary work of actual questionnaire design? We recommend starting out by consulting two kinds of people with special expertise.

EXPERTS AND INSIDERS

Professional experts

An exploratory study should take investigators out beyond their own academic or industrial subculture, to new "experts"—ones with differing counsel if at all possible. If investigators consult only the like-minded, they are likely to constrict the intellectual range of their inquiry and to give the *appearance* of bias. Academic researchers do not often have to contend with the kind of publicity that election pollsters face routinely, but when they do, they are much better prepared if they have already absorbed criticism from cultural strangers or even political "enemies." The recent attack on the Ladd-Lipset surveys of American academics by Serge Lang, a mathematician, is a complicated matter and doubtless a rare event, but Lang's charges of bias should serve as a cautionary tale to make survey researchers of all kinds more sensitive to varying interpretations of their questionnaire (Ladd and Lipset, 1976; Schuman, 1983). Survey questions, finally, must *seem fair* to people of widely different viewpoints—people one will meet, at the last, in a cross-section sample of the general population.

More important still, differing perspectives and experiences can turn up new information. Consider the finding that on three issues concerning federal government action on social policies, *conservatives* endorsed federal intervention almost as often as the sample as a whole did. The questions were of this form:

- Do you agree or disagree that the *federal government* ought to help people get medical care at low cost? [Turner and Martin, 1984, I: 82-83.]

The poll directors concluded that conservatives seemed to be moving to the left. The North American Newspaper Alliance was skeptical, however, and commissioned a split-ballot experiment that asked the "federal government" wording to half the sample, and to the other half substituted "private enterprise." The results showed that most people also favored intervention by private enterprise, and a comparable majority of *liberals* favored it, too.

Were conservatives moving to the left and liberals moving to the right? The split-ballot experiment suggested another hypothesis entirely: The public might be more concerned with getting action on these problems than with the issue of who took responsibility. This may be another illustration of agree/disagree problems that we noted in Chapter 2, but the important point for our present purposes is that the results were generated by the suspicion of bias. It is useful to be faced with these suspicions while one's questionnaire is still under construction, by intensive interviewing of professional experts on the other side of some intellectual or political fence.

Cultural insiders

Exploratory inquiry can involve "in depth" interviews with members of the target population, and it is the conviction of McKennell (1974), among others, that it should. He is skeptical of the practice of taking attitude items from "the literature," because they often represent other professionals' impression of what people in general think about things, with almost no validation by work with people in general themselves. At this exploratory stage, there is little prospect of formally *sampling* the target population, but interviewing even a few individuals can enrich the researcher's perspective. Another useful procedure is to assemble somewhat more formally the insiders of a given subculture in a "focused discussion group." This can be of special value when a target population is likely to have special perceptions, problems, and idioms that may be relatively foreign to the investigator—youth culture, gambling, drugs, prisons, and so on.

Because survey questions are now so abundant, it is the more difficult to proceed in the spirit of McKennell's (1974: 33) advice and undertake one's work "like an anthropologist approaching an alien culture, and regard one's own background and established frames of reference as a positive hindrance." Unfortunately, most of us are probably all too likely to neglect this preliminary phase of exploration and move quite directly to writing new questions and borrowing others from the survey literature.

BORROWING QUESTIONS FROM OTHERS

Large-scale surveys are now so common in American cultural and scientific life that survey questions have accumulated in a truly mountainous supply. Easy access to many survey questions is possible through various published compilations of survey questions. Early in the process of designing a questionnaire, one should consult these data, for they are very likely to save time and effort. Here we list nine that we have found most useful:

- Converse, Philip E., Jean D. Dotson, Wendy J. Hoag, and William H. McGee III (eds.), *American Social Attitudes Data Sourcebook 1947-1978* (Cambridge, MA: Harvard University Press, 1980).

- Gallup, George, *The Gallup Poll: 1935-1971* 9 vols. (New York: Random House, vols. 1-3, 1935-1971; Wilmington, DE: Scholarly Resources, Inc., vols. 4-9, 1972-1981).

- Hastings, Philip K. and Jessie C. Southwick (eds.), *Survey Data for Trend Analysis: An Index to Repeated Questions in U. S. National Surveys Held by the Roper Public Opinion Research Center* (Roper Public Opinion Research Center, 1974).

- Martin, Elizabeth, Diana McDuffee, and Stanley Presser, *Sourcebook of Harris National Surveys: Repeated Questions 1963-1976* (Chapel Hill: Institute for Research in Social Science, University of North Carolina Press, 1981).

- Miller, Warren E., Arthur H. Miller, and Edward J. Schneider, *American National Election Studies Data Sourcebook 1951-1978* (Cambridge, MA: Harvard University Press, 1980).

- National Opinion Research Center, *General Social Surveys 1972-1985: Cumulative Code Book* (Chicago: NORC, 1985).

- Robinson, John P., Robert Athanasiou, and Kendra B. Head, *Measures of Occupational Attitudes and Occupational Characteristics* (Ann Arbor, MI: Institute for Social Research, 1969).

- Robinson, John P., Jerrold G. Rusk, and Kendra B. Head, *Measures of Political Attitudes* (Ann Arbor, MI: Institute for Social Research, 1968).

- Robinson, John P., and Phillip R. Shaver, *Measures of Social-Psychological Attitudes* (Ann Arbor, MI: Institute for Social Research, 1973, rev. ed.).

Need we pretest these tried and true questions? It's a good idea, for two reasons. First, because language constantly changes, and we may catch some of these changes only if interviewers listen carefully and relay respondent comments. For example, interviewers for the National Election Study reported new meanings given this question:

- Do you think the people in Washington are smart people who know what they are doing?

This item had been used in the 1960s as one of several indicators of confidence in government. At the time of the Watergate scandals in the 1970s, however, new meaning was given to the question, as certain respondents volunteered wryly, "Oh yeah, those guys know what they're doing, all right—they're plenty smart."

Were *many* people supplying a cynical new context for "smart people"? There is rarely a means of knowing from pretests. These vignettes from the field nevertheless serve as a reminder that survey questions can weather and age with time, and some should be retired from replication. Pretesting of borrowed items is important, for a second reason, because the meaning of questions can be affected by the context of neighboring questions in the interview, as we have noted in Chapter 2.

Pretesting: Strategies, Purposes, and Phases

Pretesting a survey questionnaire is always recommended—no text in survey methods would speak against such hallowed scientific advice—

but in practice it is probably often honored in the breach or the hurry. There is never the money nor, as deadlines loom, the time, to do enough of it. There is a corollary weakness that the practice is intuitive and informal. There are no general principles of good pretesting, no systematization of practice, no consensus about expectations, and we rarely leave records for each other. How a pretest was conducted, what investigators learned from it, how they redesigned their questionnaire on the basis of it—these matters are reported only sketchily in research reports, if at all. Not surprisingly, the power of pretests is sometimes exaggerated and their potential often unrealized.

STRATEGIES OF DESIGN

A given pretest scheme projects a set of expectations for respondents, and variations in these change the character of the pretest. The design can change by whether or not respondents know that it is a pretest and by the role that interviewers play.

Respondents' awareness: participating and undeclared pretests

We term it a "participating" pretest when respondents are *told* that this is a practice run, and are asked to explain their reactions and answers. This design opens some doors of information and closes others. It opens the possibility, for example, of asking very detailed probes about each question, phrase by phrase, even key word by word.

- "What did the whole question mean to you? How would you say it?"
- "What did _____ make you think of?"
- "What was it you had in mind when you said _____?"

Because there is no need to simulate an actual interview, one can also ask respondents to react to different wordings of the same basic question.

- "Consider the same question this way: _____."
- "How would you answer that question now?"
- "You said _____. Would you feel differently if I said _____?"

With this "intensive" design, one can examine a few questions in great detail. Not a large number, or the questionnaire as a whole. The participating strategy may limit the range of possible respondents as well, because it is probably of greatest interest to people who are accustomed to surveys, reflective and confident about their own opinions and mental processes, sensitive to nuances of language, as well as willing to give up time and thought to help social scientists. Narrowed down to this subset, investigators may find themselves relying on that familiar source of forced labor—colleagues, friends, and family.

One interesting study of pretesting used respondents from the broader public (convenience samples of store customers and a random sample of households) in a variant on the participating pretest (Hunt et al., 1982). The findings raise important doubts about whether or not the general public should be asked to serve as actual judges of survey questions. In a short written questionnaire, ten questions were designed to represent five well-known faults, such as questions with incomplete alternatives, as in "Do you vote Republican or Democrat?"; and questions with inappropriate vocabulary, such as "Do you think that the current inflation is demand based or cost based?"

The researchers felt that they built in "blatant" errors and asked their subjects "to be critical," but most of their respondents found nothing much to complain about. The missing alternative error was by far the most visible: a third of the 146 respondents commented on the problem, which is probably about the proportion who needed the main missing alternative, "Independent." Inappropriate vocabulary was noticeable to a somewhat smaller group, but "loaded words," "double-barreled" questions, and ambiguous questions were virtually unnoticed by almost everyone. This rare and welcome research on the pretest suggests that respondents are not very critical or sophisticated about survey questions, even when invited to be, and their counsel may not be a very good guide to practice. (Many respondents probably answer survey questions out of basic civility and politeness). Their actual *answers*, nevertheless—their interpretations and misinterpretations of investigators' intent—are likely to be illuminating.

In what we call the "undeclared" pretest the respondent is not told that this is a questionnaire under construction, and the interviewer plays it straight. Here one can indeed probe *some* of the questions for respondents' frame of reference and meaning, but not with the intensity or exhaustiveness permitted in the participating strategy. In this more "extensive" design one can test more questions and do so in a mode closer to the final questionnaire. The best strategy is probably to begin with a participating pretest, then move to an undeclared one.

The interviewers' responsibilities

The role of interviewers in the pretest can also vary, especially in the degree to which the role is structured. Some investigators who do pretesting themselves prefer the freedom of improvising questions on the spot during a first pretest. Very skilled interviewers can be instructed to do the same thing, keeping a close record of the exact questions they asked, or tape-recording the whole encounter. The degree of structure can also vary within the same pretest, with a few key staff researchers free to depart from a structured schedule to explore leads on the spot, and most interviewers constrained to test the questionnaire as written. In another variant, all interviewers can ask some unstructured questions at the end of a standardized interview (Belson, 1981).

THE PURPOSES OF PRETESTS

The confident comment that a certain question "has been pretested" implies, first, that pretesting is a permanent state of grace—once pretested, always pretested. This in turn implies that a pretested question can be pulled out of one questionnaire and simply patched into another without losing its pretesting credentials. Neither assumption is safe. "Pretested for what?" is the appropriate query, for there are some very specific purposes. Consider these ten, the first four of which are tests for specific questions:

- variation
- meaning
- task difficulty
- respondent interest and attention

The last six bear more on the questionnaire as a whole:

- "flow" and naturalness of the sections
- the order of questions
- skip patterns

- timing
- respondent interest and attention, overall
- respondent well-being

We shall consider the two groups in turn.

Testing questions

Variation. Testing items for an acceptable level of variation in the target population is one of the most common goals of pretesting, and it is probably this purpose that people usually have in mind when they say that a question "has been pretested." Questions that show a 95/5 or 99/1 distribution of Yes/No may represent descriptive findings of capital importance if, for example, they mean that 95% of a population has learned to read and write, that 1% is at risk for a certain disease, or the like. Often, however, one is on the lookout for items showing greater variability that will be useful in detecting subgroups of people or clusters of attitudes of analytic interest. One rarely has enough pretest cases to be at all confident, but very skewed distributions from a pretest can at least serve as warning signals.

Meaning. For this purpose, the fact that an item has been used in a published study may not tell whether it was ever fully pretested for meaning; or whether the meaning intended by the investigator was shared by most respondents at the time; or if so, whether it *still* is. If the original source was a written questionnaire administered to college students, it should be considered with special suspicion, and duly pretested for its applicability to a general population. The literature offers some colorful examples of confusion—"profits" taken for "prophets" is a classic—and other pretest vignettes provide other merry examples: "heavy traffic in the neighborhood" meaning trucks to investigators and drugs to respondents; "family planning" meaning birth control to investigators and saving money for vacations to other people (Berckmans, 1985). One woman of whom we recently asked family social-class level—"poor, working class, middle class, etc."—told us that her family wasn't really very sociable. How many people brought quite a different meaning to "social class" than the one we intended? Very few, as we happily learned from pretest results, but it was worth checking.

Testing the meaning of questions is probably the most important pretesting purpose. It may nevertheless be the most neglected because it can require such extensive probing, as in Belson's ambitious tests of questions. He administered, first, a short questionnaire to four small quota samples of approximately 50 each on the subject of television, using questions of a sort that he found in frequent use by a set of market researchers. The day after the interview, a specially trained interviewer returned to conduct a second intensive interview on the meaning of the questions.

On the face of it, the results are appalling. In no case did all respondents bring to every part of the question the approximate meaning intended by the investigator. For the highest scoring question, 50% of the sample interpreted all parts of the question within acceptable meanings. In the lowest-scoring question, *nobody* did. The average, overall, was an unimpressive 29%. The fact that Belson selected problem questions, however—types that he expected to confuse respondents— makes his findings a little less grim.

Belson's findings, nonetheless, carry two very important messages. First, the meaning that investigators intend for many questions actually used in surveys is often not the meaning that respondents apprehend. Respondents do not necessarily even *hear* every word of the question, much less assume the definitions that the investigator has in mind, or fully understand the concepts. Although a question presents the word "impartial," for example, perhaps the "im" gets lost and the respondent hears a synonym for biased, or perhaps the word "impartial" itself is an unfamiliar one (Belson, 1981: 76-86).

Second, respondents nevertheless answer most questions because, as Belson (1981: 371) writes,

> When a respondent finds it difficult to answer a question, he is likely to modify it in such a way as to be able to answer it more easily.

This is the first of 15 hypotheses that Belson distills from his results. For our reading, it is the most important and the most general of them all, and in fact many of the others could be subsumed under it. Respondents probably modify questions, for the most part, not because they are lazy or want to hide their ignorance, or even because surveys project a demand to be opinionated, as Riesman and Glazer (1948) cogently observed over 35 years ago. People seem to answer questions, most importantly, because they expect survey questions—or at least survey interviewers—to be sensible; people *think* they heard the question properly; or the part of the question that is meaningful takes on more salience or vividness and they answer that part; or they take the parts that are meaningful and reassemble a different question from them and answer that. In sum, respondents probably *transform* obscure questions into ones that seem sensible from their standpoint as they strain for meaning.

Task difficulty. A question can be hard to answer even though the meaning is entirely clear if the respondent has not previously packaged the information in the way the question demands. "How many pounds of coffee have you consumed this past year?" may be an answerable question for some very methodical shoppers, but most of us do not total up our consumption of coffee by the year, or even by the pound, and our estimate in these terms would probably be quite unreliable. The literature about "non-attitudes" should help us avoid asking respondents things they know little about (Converse, 1970; Smith, 1984a)—but it continues to be easy, nevertheless, to ask people questions we want to know rather than ones they are able to answer.

Take a recent DAS question:

- How important has it been to you to have more money than your parents had—very important, somewhat important, or not very important?

From a few follow-up probes, we learned that the question triggered people's ruminations about the importance of money itself ("money doesn't buy happiness," and so on) often without reference to their parents' fortunes, as if the question had read:

- How important has it been to you to have more money? . . . Very important, somewhat important, or not very important?

It seems to have been an evocative question for people who had been very poor as children; for others who had no such vivid memories, however, the whole idea may have been quite new. A few of our respondents volunteered just that. "Why I never thought of it before—I guess I'd have to say Not Very Important."

There are two morals to the money story. One turns on retrospective measurement itself, which is rarely recommended, because it is known that recall even of dramatic events can be fragile: People may forget the event itself or they may misremember the time at which the event occurred. And yet retrospective measures are sometimes essential. We asked a number of retrospective questions in this particular study, without illusion that we were getting exact measures of the past; for reasons connected to the analysis we were willing to take the risk of rough approximations.

There are, indeed, such times when any "rules" of question writing will be bent, because at the time it seems rather a matter of Hobson's choice. In this case, however—and this is the second moral—we did not pretest this question well enough. It was only on the final questionnaire that we picked up a smattering of evidence that many people had not organized the past or compared it with the present in quite the way we were assuming. Had we gotten the cues earlier, we might well have added an open-ended probe to the question on the final questionnaire to distinguish systematically the people for whom the question was a meaningful one. Or dropped the question.

Respondent interest and attention. This is an aspect of pretesting that ordinarily seems to get rather short shrift. Investigators are rather prone to forgetting that not everyone brings the same fervent interest to their topic that they do. Interviewers usually know whether respondents seem interested or stimulated by the questionnaire, and should be asked to report systematically on this dimension, at least to note questions that respondents found especially interesting and especially dull.

There is little research to support such caution. In fact, the proposition that survey data deteriorate when respondents' attention and interest flag markedly is one we take largely on faith and the evidence of fatigue effects in learning experiments. There is some recent suggestive evidence that such things hold in surveys, too. In a self-administered questionnaire, Herzog and Bachman (1981) asked some fairly large sets of questions in the same format; as many as 23 items were grouped together with a four-point choice ranging from Strongly Agree to Strongly Disagree. This format would probably have been more monotonous and deadly in a personal interview than in this paper-and-pencil questionnaire, but there was evidence of a "fatigue" effect toward the end of the question sets, as respondents tended to check the same alternative, no matter what the question.

Still, research into fatigue or boredom effects in surveys is rare—and it is a more complicated matter than the sheer length of time required by the questionnaire. Sharp and Frankel's (1983) recent study shows that length of the interview is experienced by respondents as a negative factor but is not in fact predictive of their willingness to participate in subsequent interviews. In the design of questions, investigators usually try to avoid the wearing repetition. They make of their surveys something of a pastiche, one kind of questioning and then another; a bit of so-and-so's format, and something in another style. This is an aspect of survey design that is guided by mysterious matters: the "art" of writing and especially arranging survey questions to keep respondents' attention and interest. Varying the format is important. In personal interviews, one can do this not only by using different kinds of oral questions but also by using some "show cards" or a small booklet that lists answer alternatives and some self-administered questions, but on the telephone one's choices are more restricted. Here, especially, one must pretest carefully for a desirable balance between the benefits of question variety and the "start-up" costs of explaining a new question format.

The first four objectives that we have discussed bear especially on the testing of *questions*. Another set of purposes that we turn to now bears more on the *questionnaire as a whole*. We should not put too fine a point on this distinction, for in every phase of pretesting, one is tinkering with the wording and form of specific questions and also trying to cast the overall shape of the questionnaire. Still, there is a difference in emphasis. One cannot really test the questionnaire as a whole until the basic sections are chosen and arranged in a given order, with the wording of many questions cast in more or less final form. So the pretesting objectives for the questionnaire tend to come second.

Pretesting the questionnaire

"Flow" and naturalness. Testing the "flow" of the questionnaire is such a matter of intuitive judgment that it is hard to describe or codify. One can at least be guided by one crucial caveat: Reading is not enough. One must listen to the questionnaire, over and over, hearing it as interviewers actually deliver it, trying to hear it as respondents do, always mindful that they will *not* have the print in front of them to review and clarify the meaning. What respondents hear is what they get, and every question probably comes anew to respondents, with a certain "surprise" quality.

The interest and clarity of the questions and a "sensible" arrangement probably contribute more to a coherent flow than any very elaborate transitions from section to section. Transitions can be simple and brief, such as "Now I am going to ask you some questions about your job . . . " or even the vague preparation, "Now I have some questions on a different topic . . . " These are not very elegant transitions, but in our experience they do not have to have nor should there be many of them. One wants a few (redundant) words that slow things down enough for the interviewer and the respondent to turn a corner to another subject—now and then, when without a transitional phrase changes seem too sharp.

The order of questions. The positive guides to the order of questions are few, and bear only the credentials of common sense. The proposition that one should open the questionnaire with "interesting" questions, for instance, seems like a good idea—assuming of course that one has tested questions for their interestingness.

Frey (1983: 103-105) offers more specific counsel that in telephone interviewing, especially, the initial questions should be items directly related to the topic of the interview expressed in the introductory statement, as in this example:

Hello. This is ———— calling from the Telephone Survey Center of the University of Nevada, Las Vegas. We are conducting a survey of Nevada residents on their opinions and perceptions of the quality of life in the state. . . .

First, I would like to ask how you feel about Nevada as a place to live. Do you consider it Very Desirable, Somewhat Desirable, Somewhat Undesirable, or Very Undesirable?

Frey suggests following this with an open-ended "Why" question of this sort: "What specifically do you find (desirable/undesirable) about living in Nevada?" to allow the respondent "to find his or her 'telephone voice.'" His basic point about the opening question is that if the introduction has successfully aroused the respondent's interest, it can be just as quickly deflated by a question unrelated to the announced topic, such as "Did you vote in the last national election?" or "What is your race?" Because we know that respondents' answers to open-ended questions tend to be more terse on the telephone than they are face-to-face (Groves and Kahn, 1979), finding a "telephone voice" may be of some special value. We would nevertheless urge caution in using open-ended questions with any frequency at the beginning *if* the questionnaire is basically closed, for one is "training" the respondent in the questionnaire from the very outset. In addition, open questions can sometimes be quite demanding, and tasks at the beginning of the interview should be easy ones that do not tax or discourage the respondent.

It is common practice to put "background" questions at the end of the interview. This ritual reflects, most of all, the sensitivity of income questions, which are the most vulnerable to refusal. If respondents are offended by being asked their income, at least their negative reaction appears late in the questionnaire. Most background questions are not really sensitive, however, and they are usually fairly easy for the respondent to answer and can be something of a welcome set of questions if earlier questions have been fairly demanding.

It may not be necessary, however, to move all background questions to the end of the questionnaire just because the income questions may belong there. Putting some background questions up front can be of use if the survey topic bears closely on the individual's own life history and experience, and the approach of the questionnaire is largely chronological. Moreover, if the interview is broken off before completion, some basic background information has been obtained. NORC's General Social Survey divides background questions between the beginning and the end of the interview for these reasons.

Skip patterns. Questionnaires must be pretested not only for the usual typographical errors, but for the logic and format of skip patterns, which can be very complex. If the skip patterns are incorrect or ambiguous, interviewers may vault over various questions or even whole sections and leave unanticipated holes in the data. Defective skip patterns should be caught before pretesting so that pretest interviewers can concentrate on the questions and the respondents' reactions rather than having to struggle against bad skips to get the questionnaire read at all.

The best way of proofreading the skip patterns is to turn the task over to several individuals, each of whom follows the route for a certain "scenario," such as these:

(A) The respondent was born in Mexico in 1947 and came to the U.S. in 1966. This is her first marriage; her husband had two children by a previous marriage, who are now living with R and her husband. She first voted in the 1976 national election . . .

(B) The respondent, age 56, has worked at an automobile assembly plant for 11 years as manager of the shipping department. He is married, without children. He and his wife have recently bought into an investment partnership that is buying real estate in Florida, and they hope to retire there when he is 62 . . .

Dividing up the labor in this way is useful for finding logical errors in the skip patterns. People who are sophisticated about surveys in general but uninformed about this one are especially valuable for this assignment, for they will duly follow the road signs of the questionnaire. Staff members who have been involved in designing the study may tend to go where they are "supposed" to go whether the skip directs them there or not.

It is important to think of the questionnaire as a road map, and consider its graphics accordingly. If the skip pattern is at all ambiguous visually, an interviewer may take the wrong route; and then confident that this is the correct way, never carefully read that instruction again. The clearest instructions are strong arrows, lines, outlines, very boxy boxes, with no fine print and no extraneous instructions at all.

Timing. It is ordinarily useful to ask interviewers to time each part of the questionnaire, section by section. That face-to-face survey interviews should average no more than a scant hour is a norm of practice with little grounding in experiment, though it has a long tradition in the 50-minute hour of clinical therapy and college classroom instruction. Beyond that time, one begins to worry about respondent fatigue, interview break-off, and initial refusal if respondents know the expected length. For telephone interviewing, the norms are for shorter times.

Respondent interest and attention, overall. Interviewers should be encouraged to notice and report on respondents' interest in the study. The problem may indeed be that the whole questionnaire is simply too long, and, if so, there is probably no better remedy than going back to the cutting board. Two other prescriptions should be considered, as well: new content and task variety.

Investigators will be loath to give any room to "throwaway" questions (without prospective analytic value) just because respondents might like to talk about them. With field costs so high, this is luxury beyond the typical research purse. Yet it is also foolish to expect respondents to have high motivation and sustained attention for a questionnaire that does not take much account of their interests. We do well to consider the questionnaire now and then from the respondents' perspective: Where is it lively and responsive? Where is it slow going? Can we go a little further to meet them halfway? Can we add anything that serves our own analytic direction and also brightens the way for respondents? At the least, we may have to place some questions strategically to perk up lagging interest.

The liveliest questionnaires in our ken move respondents from one activity to another, as they proceed through the questionnaire. Respondents are asked a set of Yes/No questions, perhaps; then a group of questions involving one choice from a list of, say, five options; then they are asked several questions in which they rate their own feelings on a scale; then they choose between one idea or the other. And so on. The variety of the answering task has been designed to engage the respondent's active attention. This characteristic can be pretested, by asking interviewers to make systematic observations of respondents' interest, and by asking respondents to report their reactions for themselves. Task variety cannot captivate respondents if the subject matter itself is irretrievably difficult or dull, for content itself appears to be far more telling. Questionnaires bearing on people's own experiences, life histories, and health are predictably more interesting to most people than an exclusive focus on attitudes or information. But when investigators want to explore topics that are not likely to be of widespread appeal, task variety may well be of special importance.

Respondent well-being. In our time surveys have burgeoned far beyond the original realms of political polling. Survey interviewers are now admitted into realms of privacy and sensitivity, to ask questions about alcoholism, drugs, crime, heterosexual and homosexual experience, marital satisfaction, divorce, abuse, the death of children, loneliness, mental illness, depression, suicide, physical handicaps, widowhood, terminal illness, religious experience, anxiety, and faith. The litany is long. Survey researchers have proved a voracious lot, with a huge appetite for information about people's lives and experiences.

Are people sufficiently protected from possible injury in this research process? Requirements that surveys offer "informed consent" to their respondents and undergo "human subjects review" by their institution represent an effort to protect respondents from any untoward effects. There are real problems and dilemmas in these efforts, however. In surveys contracted by and for the federal government, for example, questionnaires themselves are reviewed, and this means that they must be put in final form months before the field work is started, which is a major block to the research process. In the university, on the other hand, a "human subjects review" of the overall research proposal is usually undertaken months before a questionnaire is even designed; it is our impression that there is unlikely to be any review of the final questionnaire at all.

In the academic setting, who can say that a questionnaire is distressing respondents, leaving them feeling worse about themselves or their lives than the interviewer found them? If that happened, would the investigators know? Who would tell them? Is it anyone's responsibility to find out?

In our own experience, interviewers have sometimes taken that role. In a recent project, long-term and very skilled professional interviewers insisted that the questionnaire needed major redesigning. The topic was psychological depression, and interviewers reported that the pretest was *depressing* people with its exclusive focus on life's bad news and symptoms of mental illness. The design had included only those life events hypothesized to predict depression—the tragic and troubled and stressor events. The interviewers' intelligent reports and impressive experience finally prevailed: The questionnaire was duly redesigned to allow some upbeat features, such as the inclusion of some good life events and questions about how respondents had coped with their problems. The happy ending is that after the document went through *five* pretests, both respondents and interviewers registered great satisfaction with the study: a real favorite.

We have no hard data to support these moves. We were personally convinced that the problem was a real one by the particular interviewers' experience, arguments, concern—and talent. The experience pointed up the fact that some professional interviewers bring a personal involvement and a professional commitment to the well-being of respondents. When this is combined with personal self-confidence, broad professional experience, and good judgment, their advocacy on behalf of the respondent can be of enormous value to the quality of a survey. Some student interviewers, even though less experienced, bring equivalent talents and sensitivities. But temporary interviewers, who are on deck for a single study, even if they have advanced training in other fields, will usually lack that special advocacy of the respondent.

PHASES OF PRETESTING

Pretests represent a "qualitative" stage in the quantitative survey enterprise, with N's nothing like what they should be for quantitative evidence. For small pretests, numbering 25-75 cases, is it really worth coding the data and hand-tallying or grinding out marginal distributions? Yes—at the upper ranges, anyway. On rare occasions, marginal distributions can provide a measure of support for certain "hunches," and diminish one's confidence in others. And they can provide some corrections. The experience of interviewing even a single real and unforgettable character, for instance, can be so vivid and compelling that staff members may come back from the field with very broad, entirely unwarranted conclusions about the questionnaire based on the infamous N of 1. A larger set of pretest interviews per person is desirable—5, for instance, would be much better. If this cannot be undertaken, quantitative data may help pretesters realize that their own experience was not entirely representative or general. And sometimes the live testimony of other interviewers who have just as vivid, entirely contrary views can help, too. In any case, both the colorful vignettes and some numbers can be useful. If interviewers' reports are often more instructive than the marginal frequencies (and in our experience, that has usually been the case), it is another indication of pretesting's qualitative hallmarks: small Ns, samples of convenience, hypothesis testing by hunch and judgment. Pretests would seem to be absolutely necessary even if almost never sufficient.

Just as most pretesting Ns are regrettably small, the number of pretest trials is often sharply limited—often to one. For a new study, to which investigators bring no previous hands-on experience, a minimum of *two* pretests is indispensable, in our view. For as we have already stressed, in a first trial the wording of the questions themselves is still uncertain enough—they are the focus of the testing—that the questionnaire does not yet have a very coherent shape. In the discussion that follows, we assume this minimum of two pretests. We will consider them in the framework of these three topics, developmental pretest I, evaluation, and polishing pretest II, and set forth some useful properties of each phase.

Developmental Pretest I

Most questions should be closed. Closed questions should generally be given the lion's share of the first pretest simply because they must generally be given the lion's share of the final interview schedule—and this is a pretest of it. To make that statement is to face one of the sternest limitations of survey research. Closed survey questions inevitably simplify and stylize the life and thought of individuals, even for the most routine of measures.

Try marital status, for instance, or number of times married. Reliably, the boxes (precoded responses) will not capture everyone's condition in a way that guides the selection of questions (skip patterns) in the rest of the questionnaire. For example, in most cases, this will be a straightforward sequence:

(A2) First, I would like to know your current marital status—are you now married, separated, divorced, or widowed, or have you not married?

(IF RESPONDENT IS DIVORCED, TURN TO PAGE 18)

But what of the man who is divorced from his first wife but lives with her and considers her his wife? He is certainly not Separated or Widowed, but is he Married, Divorced, or both? Legally, of course, he is divorced, but that does not solve our problem. Shall we ask him the questions to be asked of divorced people, or the questions to be asked of married people, or all of both?

Anyone who has conducted or coded a fair number of survey interviews knows that human experience is much too unruly in its diversity to be fully contained by the precoded responses of closed questions. When this richness thrusts out of the boxes, like so much jungle growth, we hastily set up another box, the residual "Other," and by relegating these wondrously oddball situations into this miscellaneous junk box, we lose entirely the vividness and "life" of individual character and unusual circumstance. There is little for it. Open-ended questions are far better for capturing those details and idiosyncrasies; entirely unstructured interviews conducted by master interviewers are better still; biographies and novels, of course, are probably best of all.

One repairs to closed questions for several good reasons. The first reason, and best, is that some boxes can be built to accommodate almost all cases. Our codes for marital status clearly did not cover everyone, but they covered *almost* everyone, which is not only good enough but absolutely splendid.

Another good reason is cost. To oversimplify the choices, one can pay interviewers to spend two hours with 250 respondents or less than one hour each with 500 persons. With the two-hour version, interviewers can ask and transcribe much more "in depth" detail, but an N of 250 will be too small to support any very compelling analysis. (The sampling error will be large for an N of 500, at that.) To undertake any statistical analysis at all, one will inevitably pare away much of the detail gathered in those two hours back to the bone of gross code categories. This risks a kind of triple squander of survey materials: one will pay to gather the detail (sacrificing a larger N in the process), then shear much of it away, paying for the time that takes too.

An even better reason for closed questions bears on validity. One may seek open-ended material in the very quest for greater validity, but the choice can sometimes work the other way around when the frame of reference for open questions is ambiguous. It is difficult to keep open questions free of the "tacit assumption" that Paul Lazarsfeld noted 50 years ago, with an example that remains one of our favorites. When school children in Austria were asked in an open-ended questionnaire item what they would most like to have in life, they wrote down economic and psychological goals such as big farms, good jobs, money, happiness. Nobody mentioned intelligence. When this alternative was included in a closed version of the question, it was a great favorite. The children had apparently assumed that the open question included only the goods that might be had for the striving, not the gifts of personal endowment (Jenkins, 1935: 355). There are other strengths and weaknesses about both open and closed questions that we have considered in Chapter Two. Suffice it here to say that one is well-advised to include many closed questions in Pretest I and probe their meaning in open ended follow-ups. Because open questions will usually constitute at most a small part of the interview schedule, they must be selected and trimmed with great care.

Rough codes for open questions should be designed in advance. In the press of field deadlines, it is usually difficult to find time to anticipate codes for open questions; but even if this preliminary code construction is done in a rather informal and approximate fashion, it enhances the realism of the first pretest and the particular value of any open questions used. It has the great value of helping investigators face up to what their objectives are in asking the question at all. And explaining the question objectives is essential for the interviewer, for without this information, the interviewer cannot know when a question has been answered.

The first pretest interview should be less than twice the final expected length. This is merely to say that the first pretest can be rather outsize, as long as one can also conduct a second pretest. A first pretest running as long as two hours can be useful, but this should be considered an absolute maximum. Beyond this length, the labor of cutting back to an hour or less will be formidable, and even if one can find respondents willing to spend two hours, the test of some questions may be doubtful if the length of the interview has tired them and dulled their attention and interest. Such a long trial may be testing personal endurance more than anything more cogent. If there is only one pretest in view, it should be much shorter: one should strive to make it an hour and a quarter as a maximum. Remember, too, that interviewers conducting a pretest may have to do most of their work in the evenings, and a long pretest may restrict them to one interview per evening; and in that case, the time scheduled for pretesting will have to be stretched.

Respondents should resemble the target population. A probability sample of the survey's target population would make an ideal pretest. But this is ordinarily much too expensive. One must nevertheless take a pretest out beyond the small worlds of colleagues, friends, or family, who offer much too thin a slice of life. Interviewers should not be left to their own devices. In a recent pretest conducted by DAS students, we found that almost half of our respondents were graduate students, hardly a cross section of the population.

There are two likely routes out of the small world. One way is to take advantage of group character or neighborhood stratification of importance to the study: One can go door-to-door in neighborhoods that are visibly ethnic, or elderly, or young and noisy with children, and so forth. A second is to interview strangers, by knocking on doors close to home or work. This seems an absolute minimum for pretesting. Going this route will ordinarily not yield as heterogeneous a collection of respondents as the first way, but it will certainly be more useful than interviewing one's own friends and relatives. (It seems fair to insist that interviewing in that inner circle should simply *not count* as a pretest.) If one is pretesting by telephone, one, of course, has no visual cues to heterogeneity, but one can achieve something of the same effect by selecting central office codes (the first three digits following the area code) that are known to span a range of neighborhoods, though one will unfortunately not be able to identify the neighborhoods themselves. One can also make a random selection of telephone numbers within those codes, staying within a close radius to save money and relaxing selection rules to save time.

A pretest N of 25-75 is reasonable. The Magic N for a pretest is of course as many as you can get. We see 25-75 as a valuable pretest range, which can vary first with the experience and talent of the interviewers. With student interviewers, one may have to settle for a yield of 2-3 interviews each. This is not an optimal number per individual but at least the task is manageable and each interviewer's share of the variance is appropriately small, both features of special value when the interviewers are inexperienced.

With experienced professional interviewers, the N usually has to be smaller because of costs, and in the best circumstances we think it safely can be. NORC's interviewing staff, for example, is ordinarily not augmented by student trainees, and the recommendation by Sheatsley (1983) that the N can range around 10-25 probably reflects that fact. SRC's practice is similar: Pretest Ns in recent years have averaged about 30, with a half dozen interviewers each conducting about 5 interviews. Even modest pretests of this order of magnitude have value for undergirding intuitive judgments with at least a jot of data and with the informed impressions of experienced pretest interviewers.

From the sizes we have been considering—an N of 25 with professional interviewers; an N of 50 or more with students—one might infer that professionals can be twice as effective as students for pretest work. That is not implausible, if the professional interviewers are selected for their pretesting skill and are an experienced, motivated elite of their group. A student group may well be the more highly educated, to be sure, but it is also likely to vary more in the interest, motivation, and talent for survey interviewing per se. Some students turn up in a survey practicum, after all, because they have to fulfill an academic requirement, not because they have any special interest, gift, or stamina for field work. Experienced professional interviewers who survive the winnowings are, to some extent at least, self-selected for just those qualities.

Two issues about who should conduct pretests: The first issue is whether or not pretest interviewers should represent the best of the professional staff, or the full range of talent that will ultimately work on the study. The DeMaio research group (1983), among others, favors using the full range. They feel that the most able interviewers can make even a poor schedule "work," and may not reveal the problems that a flawed schedule will present for some of the less able interviewers on the staff.

There are no data that we know to support one view or another, but our own experience argues for choosing the most talented pretesting interviewers. They tend to be strong advocates for their respondents' right to clear, sensible, interesting questions, and they spot questionnaire defects with a good deal of zest, yea, even dedicated nit-picking. The best professional interviewers are not loath to teach investigators, and in many instances their spirited counsel has been very valuable indeed. It should be noted that even among the most competent, experienced interviewers, pretesting is not everyone's cup of tea. Those with a special interest and flair for pretesting can not only catch poor designs, but also make extraordinarily good suggestions for revision (Flanagan, 1985). But this luxurious choice will be beyond the reach of many survey investigators, who will not have easy access or sufficient funds to hire professional interviewers for pretesting. In that case, everyone will be pressed into pretesting duty, whether especially talented for interviewing or not.

The second issue turns on whether or not investigators should be among them. Some writers feel that the research staff should not participate in pretesting unless they are skilled in standard interviewing techniques. Others feel that the field experience can be of value even without that training. We side with the latter. If investigators are poor interviewers, they do not need to conduct the questionnaire themselves; they can see how their questionnaire works in the field by going along with a better interviewer. Or at the very least, they can listen in on telephone interviews. Direct pretesting experience can make investigators more sensitive and sympathetic to the rigors of the interviewers' task, as well as knowledgeable (and humble) about the frailty of their questions. It is our impression that not enough researchers get their own feet wet and weary in the field.

Evaluating pretests

We have sketched out some design features for Pretest I, but these alone do not suggest how to make the best use of the pretest experience. The following six procedures all can offer something of value:

- marginal comments on the schedule
- oral debriefing
- written reports (section by section of questionnaire)
- written questionnaires (specific facets or problems)
- field observation of the questionnaire in action
- coding of answers and tallying of marginal frequencies

It is only the last two that do not depend directly on the observations of interviewers. The DeMaio group (1983: 119) has noted that:

Interviewers are a key and often underrated element in the practice of survey research. They constitute the link between respondents and researchers, and in their direct contact with respondents, they can pick up valuable information which may be of interest to questionnaire designers.

As they say, "the systematic exploration of an interviewer's knowledge has been seriously neglected in the literature." In our own experience, that knowledge has been indispensable. Except where pretests are large in size and experimental in design, thereby making possible some statistical analysis, interviewers have a virtual monopoly on the prime information.

Copious comments written in the margins of the schedule should be encouraged. At this stage, the more the better. Interviewers can be asked to give a running account of their own impressions of the interview and of all respondent comments. Interviewers vary a good deal in their ability to do this—at the very least, it takes fast writing and the ability to seize instantly upon dialogue—so one cannot expect a rich running record from everyone. But from those who can do this kind of detailed transcription, investigators can mine evidence of problems and misinterpretations, and interviewers can go back to these marginal notes for the preparation of more systematic reports.

Oral debriefing, a group discussion with interviewers very soon after the pretest, has the advantage of immediacy: Interviewers can report while their memory of the experience is quick and their interest, usually, high. (The hazards of debriefing are those of any undisciplined discussion—if the best raconteurs or the more dominant personalities swamp the meeting and inhibit some of the less voluble interviewers from reporting their experiences at all; and the meeting should be structured accordingly.) It is not inexpensive to bring a set of professional interviewers together for what may well be a half-day's discussion, but we have found it money well spent.

Written comments may be fruitful, alone or in conjunction with a debriefing. When we have required written comments from student interviewers, we have sometimes collated the comments by topic, duplicated them, and given the entire set back to the students. The purpose has been to economize on academic class time; the schedule of the practicum was crowded enough, on occasion, that we had little time for debriefing; and given that constraint, it seemed important to provide feedback about *everyone's* experiences, so that individual students would not overgeneralize from their own. In any case, written reports have made for easy and systematic reference in revising the questionnaire.

We have also sometimes used both written reports and oral debriefing together. This has actually proved rather repetitive, for interviewers have tended to offer in discussion the same points that they make in writing. This may be a minor disadvantage, however, if the two reporting forms, in conjunction, enhance interviewers' interest and morale, while also providing useful pretest evaluation. And the combination has seemed to work that way.

A *questionnaire* can be a useful way to communicate with a far-flung interviewing staff. For example, questions such as these can serve as a useful focus for interviewer comments:

Questionnaire for Interviewers

Please make out a separate questionnaire for each pretest interview you conduct. For all "yes" answers, please specify the *question numbers* or section and *explain* what the situation or problem seemed to be.

(1) Did any of the questions seem to make R uncomfortable?

(2) Did you have to repeat any questions?

(3) Did R misinterpret any questions?

(4) Which questions were the most difficult or awkward for you to read? Have you come to dislike any specific questions? Why?

(5) Did any of the sections seem to drag?

(6) Were there any sections in which you felt that the respondent would have liked the opportunity to say more?

And so on. The specific questions of interest will depend, of course, on the survey and its particular problems.

Field observation of pretest interviewers, which comes highly recommended by the DeMaio group, allows an interviewer to give his or her entire attention to the conduct of the interview itself, while another person is free to listen to and observe how the questionnaire is working. Observation is sometimes practiced by field supervisors but it can be valuable for survey investigators (DeMaio, 1983: 101). Another variant is organizing pairs of interviewers (professionals or students) who work together during a pretest, taking turns as interviewer and observer. They can submit a joint report, concentrating their comments exclusively on properties of the questionnaire, without relaying any evaluation of each other as interviewers. Inexperienced interviewers may be more comfortable working this way in the beginning. They may learn more about the questionnaire and contribute more to its revision if they feel more confident interviewing in the presence of a peer observer than they would with a field supervisor or survey investigator. Berckmans (1985) reports some beneficial training experiences from the pairing of experienced and inexperienced interviewers.

Coding of responses, and preparation of marginal frequencies can provide a quick summary of variation. With a small pretest N, hand tallying of the closed question responses may be perfectly serviceable, and the open-ended answers can be quick coded for just a few gross categories, or even just an indication (yes/no) that the respondent interpreted the question as intended. With more substantial Ns, it may be more practical to edit the interviews quickly for direct data entry into a microcomputer.

Coding also can be used in a more ambitious way, as a part of interviewer training, to sensitize interviewers to the problems of coding and analysis that are created by poor interviewing. We usually have students code two or three pretest interviews just as a part of the practicum, to familiarize them with coding itself, and to get the work done. With the hope that the coding experience will sharpen sensitivity and skill in interviewing, we assign to student interviewers the coding of each other's pretest questionnaires. At least some then experience the plagues that poor interviewing visits upon coders, such as illegible handwriting, careless editing, poor probing; and we hope they take away the appropriate moral. For gathering data on occupation, familiarity with coding has come to seem essential. We suspect that many interviewers continue to ask occupation questions quite poorly until they have some experience or exercises in occupational coding. Experience reported by Hauser and Featherman (1977) supports that view.

Pretest II: the polishing pretest

The second pretest should be a "dress rehearsal" of the questionnaire as a whole. Pretest II is not a time to repair gross errors, or to make new exploration. It is rather a time for cutting, trimming, splicing, rearranging, and filling in new skip patterns, formatting for clarity—polishing.

As a dress rehearsal, the polishing pretest must necessarily be an undeclared one, which will be handled as a real interview. One *aspires* to produce a Pretest II schedule that is ready for the printer or final form on the computer (for Computer Assisted Telephone Interviewing). It has never worked quite that way in our experience—one always learns new information from a polishing pretest and revises accordingly—but one learns more from Pretest II by trying to make it as close as possible to the final questionnaire.

Because Pretest II is now a slimmer model, one can now ask outsiders to criticize a draft of it before it goes into the field, just as one asks colleagues to criticize academic papers in draft. The first pretest questionnaire is usually too fat to circulate (and may risk embarrassment, at that). It may be an imposition to ask colleagues to read it, and they probably cannot be much help at this point anyway, for the sheer bulk of the schedule may blur its main intellectual lines and certainly its formatting structure. (One can hardly expect to format completely a questionnaire that still has to be cut by some 50%.) But one can ask knowledgeable colleagues to read and criticize a draft of a polishing pretest, especially if one presents it along with the set of research objectives that are being operationalized. (Would that colleagues needed nothing more than the questions we present to deduce perfectly our research purposes.)

We have found our best critics to be colleagues interested in the subject matter who have, themselves, done some survey work in the area, and field or coding directors who have experience with a variety of survey questionnaires. The latter especially have shown a fine eye for the design properties of a questionnaire that affect production interviewing and production coding. The problem is time: finding a hole in the survey schedule that is big enough to get a draft out to colleagues and back with comments. When we have not found that time before Pretest II, we have asked colleagues to criticize a draft of the final questionnaire. Earlier is of course better when changes are less disruptive.

Collegial criticism is a new feature of preparing Pretest II. In other respects, the characteristics that were desirable for Pretest I are now almost mandatory: for example, most questions should be closed; code categories for the few open questions should be at least loosely sketched out in advance; respondents should be strangers who resemble the target population; the N should be around 25-75, and more if financially and humanly possible; study staff (including students, if any) should participate in conducting the pretest, along with the best and the brightest of a professional field staff.

To evaluate the second pretest and prepare the final interview schedule, we recommend only one additional procedure. It is to keep the barrier high to any new questions. This is hard discipline. Inevitably, after two pretests, study staff will have some new brainstorms. To fend off these last-minute inspirations, we have tried to stick by a rule that any new question must be given an independent test with some minimum number of respondents. This is not, finally, a thorough test of the question, because the trial is shorn of context. But at least the rule helps to discourage the less-serious people who are unwilling to find the requisite number of respondents. One may lose some splendid ideas by keeping this barrier in place but—given the problem of incorporating untried questions into an otherwise finished questionnaire—the risk seems acceptable.

The complex matter of how the final questionnaire is put into action in the field is beyond the scope of this book. We need only remind ourselves that a questionnaire is not writ in stone. It is *merely* a design, a plan for action and interaction; its execution depends on other directors and actors—able and motivated interviewers and field supervisors, effective procedures of quality control. This means that if investigators do not keep in touch with what is happening in the field, they can lose control of their questionnaire. But at that stage of a survey, responsibilities are always shared and sometimes diffuse, and how they are exercised will vary greatly by particular organizations. As Davis (1964: 231) has pointed out, if survey analysis is an art, it is more like architecture than sculpture or painting. The image seems apt for survey questionnaire design as well. Much painting and sculpture can finally be achieved by a single artist. Architects can make their drawings in solitary confinement, but their buildings take shape only as scores—sometimes hundreds—of other artists, craftsmen, technicians, take up the task. Survey questionnaire architects are no less dependent on all the others to carry their design into concrete form.

REFERENCES

ALEXANDER, C. S. and H. J. BECKER (1978) "The use of vignettes in survey research." Public Opinion Quarterly 42: 93-104.

ALWIN, D. F. and J. KROSNICK (1985) "The measurement of values in surveys: a comparison of ratings and rankings." Public Opinion Quarterly 49: 535-552.

BABBIE, E. R. (1973) Survey Research Methods. Belmont, CA: Wadsworth.

BELSON, W. R. (1981) The Design and Understanding of Survey Questions. Aldershot, England: Gower.

BELSON, W. R. and J. DUNCAN (1962) "A comparison of the checklist and the open response questioning systems." Applied Statistics: II: 120-132.

BERCKMANS, T. R. (1985) Personal communication.

BISHOP, G. F., R. W. OLDENDICK, and A. J. TUCHFARBER (1980a) "Experiments in filtering political opinions." Political Behavior 2: 339-369.

BISHOP, G. F., R. W. OLDENDICK, A. J. TUCHFARBER, and S. E. BENNETT (1980b) "Pseudo-opinions on public affairs." Public Opinion Quarterly 44: 198-209.

BRADBURN, N. (1983) "Response effects," in P. H. Rossi, J. D. Wright, and A. B. Anderson (eds.), Handbook of Survey Research. New York: Academic Press.

BRADBURN, N., S. SUDMAN, and Associates (1979) Improving Interview Method and Questionnaire Design. San Francisco: Jossey-Bass.

BRANNON, R. et al. (1973) "Attitude and action: a field experiment joined to a general population survey." American Sociological Review 38: 625-636.

CANNELL, C. F., L. OKSENBERG, and J. M. CONVERSE (1979) Experiments in Interviewing Techniques. Ann Arbor, MI: Institute for Social Research.

CARROLL, J. B., P. DAVIES, and B. RICHMAN (1973) The American Heritage Frequency Book. New York: American Heritage.

CONVERSE, P. E. (1970) "Attitudes and non-attitudes: continuation of a dialogue," in E. R. Tufte (ed.) The Quantitative Analysis of Social Problems. Reading, MA: Addison-Wesley.

———(1972) "Change in the American electorate," in A. Campbell and P. E. Converse (eds.) The Human Meaning of Social Change. New York: Russell Sage.

COWAN, C., L. MURPHY, and J. WIENER (1978) "Effects of supplemental questions on victimization estimates from the National Crime Survey." Proceedings of the Section on Survey Research Methods. Washington, DC: American Statistical Association.

DAHL, H. (1979) Word Frequencies of Spoken American English. Essex, CT: Verbatim.

DAVIS, J. A. (1964) "Great books and small groups: an informal history of a national survey," in P. E. Hammond (ed.) Sociologists at Work: Essays on the Craft of Social Research. New York: Basic Books.

76

77

DeMAIO, T. J. [ed.] (1983) Approaches to Developing Questionnaires, Statistical Policy Working Paper 10. Washington, DC: Office of Management and Budget.

Detroit Area Study (DAS) (1985) Questionnaire.

FINK, A. and J. KOSECOFF (1985) How to Conduct Surveys: A Step-by-Step Guide. Beverly Hills, CA: Sage.

FLANAGAN, H. (1985) Memos on pretesting. Detroit Area Study, University of Michigan. (unpublished)

FRANZEN, R. (1936) "Technical responsibilities involved in consumer research." Market Research 5: 3-7.

FREY, J. H. (1983) Survey Research by Telephone. Beverly Hills, CA: Sage.

GALLUP, G. H. (1935-1981) The Gallup Poll (9 vols). New York: Random House (1935-1971); Wilmington, DE: Scholarly Resources, Inc. (1972-1981).

GROVES, R. M. and R. L. KAHN (1979) Surveys by Telephone: A National Comparison with Personal Interviews. New York: Academic Press.

Louis Harris and Associates, Inc. (1970) The Harris Survey Yearbook of Public Opinion 1970: A Compendium of Current Attitudes. New York: Author.

————(1974) Family Finance Survey No. 2324 (Machine Readable Data File). Chapel Hill: Louis Harris Data Center, University of North Carolina.

HAUSER, R. M. and D. L. FEATHERMAN (1977) The Process of Stratification: Trends and Analysis. New York: Academic Press.

HENSON, R., C. F. CANNELL, and S. A. LAWSON (1979) "An experiment in interviewer style and questionnaire form," in Cannell et al. (eds.) Experiments in Interviewing Techniques. Ann Arbor, MI: Institute for Social Research.

HERZOG, A. R. and J. G. BACHMAN (1981) "Effects of questionnaire length on response quality." Public Opinion Quarterly 45: 549-559.

HITLIN, R. (1976) "On question wording and stability of response," Social Science Research 5: 39-41.

HOINVILLE, G., R. JOWELL, and Associates (1978) Survey Research Practice. London: Heinemann.

HUNT, S. D., R. D. SPARKMAN Jr., and J. B. WILCOX (1982) "The pretest in survey research: issues and preliminary findings." Journal of Marketing Research 19: 269-273.

HYMAN, H. and P. B. SHEATSLEY (1950) "The current status of American public opinion," in J. C. Payne (ed.) The Teaching of Contemporary Affairs. Twenty-first Yearbook of the National Council of Social Studies: 11-34.

JENKINS, J. G. (1935) Psychology in Business and Industry. New York: John Wiley.

KAHN, R. and C. F. CANNELL (1957) The Dynamics of Interviewing. New York: John Wiley.

KALTON, G., M. COLLINS, and L. BROOK (1978) "Experiments in wording opinion questions." Journal of the Royal Statistical Society Series C 27: 149-161.

KATZ, D. (1940) "Three criteria: knowledge, conviction, significance." Public Opinion Quarterly 4: 277-284.

KOHN, M. L. (1969) A Study of Values. Homewood, IL: Dorsey.

KORNHAUSER, A. and P. B. SHEATSLEY (1976) "Questionnaire construction and interview procedure," in C. Selltiz, L. S. Wrightsman, and S. W. Cook (eds.) Research Methods in Social Relations. New York: Holt, Rinehart.

KROSNICK, J. and D. F. ALWIN (forthcoming) "Response order effects in the measurement of values." Public Opinion Quarterly.

KUČERA, H. and W. N. FRANCIS (1967) Computational Analysis of Present-Day American English. Providence, RI: Brown University Press.

LADD, E. C. and S. M. LIPSET (1976) The Divided Academy: Professors and Politics. New York: Norton.

LAURENT, A. (1972) "Effects of question length on reporting behavior in the survey interview." Journal of the American Statistical Association 67: 298-305.

LENSKI, G. and J. LEGGETT (1960) "Caste, class, and deference in the research interview." American Journal of Sociology 65: 463-467.

LODGE, M. (1981) Magnitude Scaling: Quantitative Measurement of Opinions. Beverly Hills, CA: Sage

LOFTUS, E. F. and W. MARBURGER (1983) "Since the eruption of Mt. St. Helens did anyone beat you up? Improving the accuracy of retrospective reports with landmark events." Memory and Cognition 11: 114-120.

MACCOBY, E. E. and N. MACCOBY (1954) "The interview: a tool of social science," in G. Lindzey (ed.) Handbook of Social Psychology. Cambridge, MA: Addison-Wesley.

MARTIN, E. (1986) Report on the Development of Alternative Screening Procedures for the National Crime Survey. Washington, DC: Bureau of Social Science Research.

McKENNELL, A. (1974) Surveying Attitude Structures. Amsterdam: Elsevier.

MELLINGER, G. D., C. L. HUFFINE, and M. B. BALTER (1982) "Assessing comprehension in a survey of public reactions to complex issues." Public Opinion Quarterly 46: 97-109.

MILLER, W. E. and the National Election Studies (1982) Codebook, American National Election Study, 1980. Ann Arbor, MI: Inter-University Consortium for Political and Social Research.

MOSER, C. and G. KALTON (1972) Survey Methods in Social Investigation. London: Heinemann.

NETER, J. and J. WAKSBERG (1965) "Response errors in collection of expenditure data in household interviews: an experimental study." Technical Paper No. 11. Washington, DC: Bureau of Census.

NISBETT, R. E., E. BORGIDA, R. CRANDALL, and H. REED (1982) "Popular induction: information is not necessarily informative," in D. Kahneman, P. Slovic, and A. Tversky (eds.) Judgment under Uncertainty: Heuristics and Biases. Cambridge, England: Cambridge University Press.

NORPOTH, H. and M. LODGE (1985) "The difference between attitudes and nonattitudes in the mass public: just measurements?" American Journal of Political Science 29: 291-307.

PAYNE, S. L. (1951) The Art of Asking Questions. Princeton, NJ: Princeton University Press.

Public Opinion (1981) "An editors' report on the Yankelovich, Skelly and White 'mushiness index.'" 4 (April-May): 50-51.

RIESMAN, D. and N. GLAZER (1948) "The meaning of opinion." Public Opinion Quarterly 12: 633-648.

ROSSI, P. H. and A. ANDERSON (1982) "The factorial survey approach," in P. H. Rossi and S. L. Nock (eds.) Measuring Social Judgments. Beverly Hills, CA: Sage.

RUGG, D. and H. CANTRIL (1944) "The wording of questions," in H. Cantril (ed.) Gauging Public Opinion. Princeton, NJ: Princeton University Press.